FULL STEAM AHEAD

FULL STEAM AHEAD

HOW THE RAILWAYS MADE BRITAIN

PETER GINN & RUTH GOODMAN

William Collins
An imprint of HarperCollinsPublishers
1 London Bridge Street
London SE1 9GF

WilliamCollinsBooks.com

First published in Great Britain by William Collins in 2016

Full Steam Ahead was produced by Lion Television (an All3 Media company) for the BBC in partnership with the Open University.

21 20 19 18 17 16
10 9 8 7 6 5 4 3 2 1

ISBN 978-0-00-819431-4

Publishing Director: Myles Archibald
Senior Editor: Julia Koppitz
Design and layout: Guy Croton Publishing Services, Tonbridge, Kent
Production: Chris Wright

Colour reproduction by FMG
Printed and bound by Gráficas in Spain

Dedication

This book is dedicated to all the men, women and children who have given life, limb or time to the creation and preservation of Britain's railways.

CONTENTS

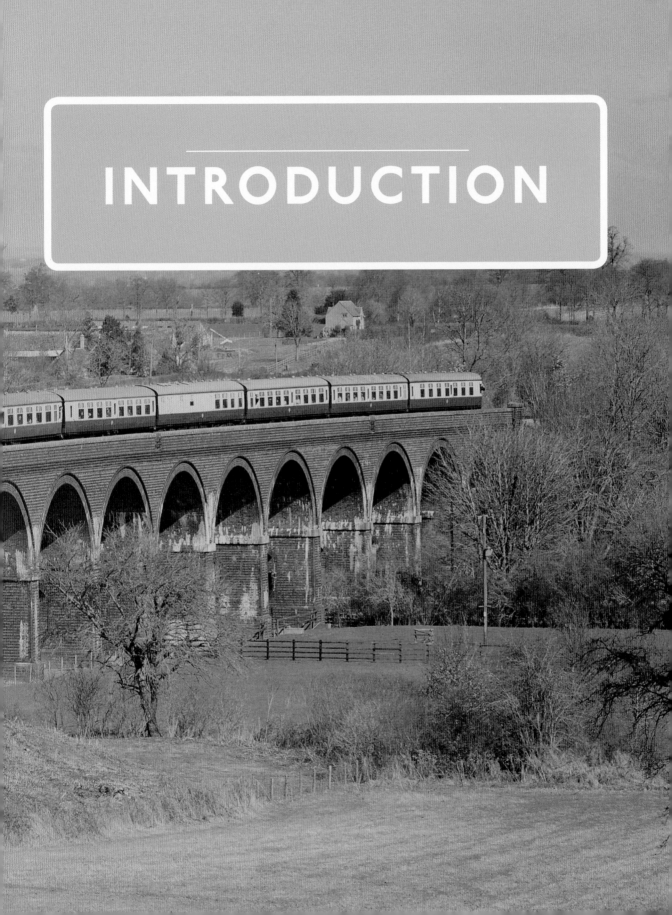

INTRODUCTION

The Victorian era was a period of immense change in Britain. It saw both the flowering and culmination of the agricultural and industrial revolutions, huge social reforms and massive technological advancements. The greatest of these was almost certainly the steam railway.

The railways changed the world. This is a bold statement, but it is unquestionably true. How scientific advancement comes about and the impact it has upon society is a complex issue. We often view our history in segments that are allocated according to the lifespans of rulers – for example, 'the Victorian era'. However, the simple fact is that we are all part of a human race that ebbs and flows as it develops and changes over an indeterminate period of time – and this process is impossible to comprehend completely as it is happening. To divide history up into segments is one step towards trying to understand it. The timeframe of the birth of the steam railways, and their subsequent development and decline, is akin to the lifespan of a human being. Therefore, the age of the steam railways is a good lens through which we can study the nineteenth and twentieth centuries.

Unlike most rulers whom periods of time are named after, the steam railways dramatically changed our lives and the lives of our ancestors. The world was already becoming a smaller place. To paraphrase Roald Dahl, at the time of the advent of the railways, there were only a couple of pages in the atlas left to fill in. The idea of using steam power was not new, but the creation of an effective engine that could convert energy into work was most certainly a massive innovation. The first steam engines had a major impact. They were big and heavy, but within reason they could be situated anywhere. Once in place, the steam engines provided power, thus reducing the need for labour. They found their calling in some factories, in agriculture and in mining.

Furthermore, railways were not a new concept. Throughout history, there has been archaeological evidence that indicates the use of trackways in various parts of the world. Also, the concept of wheels running on steel rails is not too dissimilar to that of boats travelling on canal water, when it is broken down to a basic mathematical level. Both methods of transportation reduce friction, allowing heavier loads to be pulled using less force. Just like the steam engines that pumped water out of mines, horse-drawn railways moved material from the very same mines down to the ports. However, it was the successful marriage of these two concepts that changed the world.

OPPOSITE: The Victorians were unstoppable innovators, and their era was marked by massive industrial and technological development. This is the giant waterwheel at Laxey, Isle of Man, constructed by the Casement firm in 1854.

The presenters of *Full Steam Ahead*, historians Peter Ginn, Ruth Goodman and Alex Langlands, about to board the preserved steam engine, 60103 *The Cathedrals Express*.

FULL STEAM AHEAD

In the nineteenth century, the term 'locomotive engine' was first used to distinguish a steam-powered engine that could move forwards and backwards from a completely static engine that merely provided power. Once the idea of a *moving* engine was proven to be viable, it led to a frantic creation of railways that spread across the globe. The nineteenth century saw an exponential amount of scientific development and social change, and so much of that is tied into the development of the network of railways, in both Britain and around the world.

This book has been produced to accompany the BBC 2 series *Full Steam Ahead*. In order to help ourselves examine the many and varied everyday stories from the steam railways, we divided the television programmes loosely into six themes: industry; moving people; agriculture; communication; trade; and leisure. Obviously, there is a huge overlap between each of these themes and sometimes the distinction between the programmes leaned more towards a geographical or a chronological separation. However, the themes are a good way for us to be able to focus the television programmes. It was also through dividing the various stories between each of these loose themes that we realized just how much the railways impacted on every aspect of life.

Many of the projects we have undertaken before, both for the purposes of television and for research, and have been concerned with rediscovering lost skills. Having now embarked upon a project studying the railways, we have had the chance to contextualize our work by studying the industrial side of a society that was experiencing a growing population shift from the agricultural to the urban.

Why did railways have such an impact on society? It is chiefly because of the speed of travel that they facilitated and the extent of the network that was built to support them. Not a single British railway mainline track was constructed in the twentieth century: all were created in the nineteenth century. The railways linked tiny villages and even hamlets with towns, cities and ports. Suddenly, people could pay some money for a ticket, get on a train and be in the centre of a

OVERLEAF: **Presenter Peter Ginn pictured together with the Strathspey whisky distillery team, in front of the preserved railway that serves the factory.**

"ONCE THE IDEA OF A MOVING ENGINE WAS PROVEN TO BE VIABLE, IT LED TO A FRANTIC CREATION OF RAILWAYS ACROSS THE GLOBE."

growing metropolis or in the middle of nowhere within a matter of hours or minutes. The roads had previously linked settlements together, but they were very poorly constructed and journey times

"THE WAY THAT VICTORIAN PEOPLE VIEWED SOCIETY AND INTERACTED WITH ONE ANOTHER CHANGED FOR GOOD."

were long. Relatively speaking, the railways allowed people to travel great distances in no time at all.

Much of nineteenth century industry involved the movement of great weight and bulk – huge amounts of what is collectively known as 'tonnage'. Lumps of iron, piles of coal, gallons of beer for the workers – they all needed transporting. For the first time ever, the railways enabled heavy materials to be moved quickly and on time. Yet, as much as industry built the railways, the railways built industry. This speed of movement also allowed ideas to travel quickly. Vast quantities of newspapers thundered up and down the country on trains as circulations increased and the telegraph network that accompanied the railways permitted information to be relayed at the speed of light. Something could happen in the Highlands of Scotland, be reported to a newspaper office in London, be printed and then be on sale in a shop in Aviemore, back in the Highlands, before the dust had settled. Suddenly, the whole world was moving at a pace not seen before in human history, and communications would never be the same again.

Consequently, the world became a much smaller place. Developments in the railways in Britain occurred alongside economic, social and political changes and advancements being made in America, Europe and beyond. Lessons were learned and thoughts were shared. A product designed in a small village in Wales could have a major influence on peoples' lives in northern Russia. As much as railways were pioneered in Britain, their evolution was a worldwide affair.

The way that Victorian people viewed society and interacted with one another changed for good. For a start, if it was ten o'clock in Swansea, then for the first time ever it was also ten o'clock in Newcastle. The introduction of what was known as 'railway time' saw to that (*see* page 176). The island became unified in a way that it had never been before. The speed of the new transport system also meant that no longer did

people have to seek employment close to where they lived. Trains allowed people to commute to work, for the first time ever. The railways also removed the social and economic constraint of having to grow enough food to support a local community. Food imports were nothing new, but until the railways were built, food that spoiled easily – such as fish, milk or vegetables – had to be sourced close to where a population lived. The railways could import these commodities quickly, in some instances faster than it is possible to do so today using an existing courier network. This allowed the countryside to concentrate on the cultivation of perishables and the cities no longer needed to be in easy reach of green fields or had to keep milking cows in an urban environment. Suddenly, the cities could expand and focus on industry instead of agricultural concerns.

Trains cut through impoverished urban environments and gave many their first taste of how the other half lived. This new, widespread awareness of the proliferation of urban slums in Victorian Britain prompted much of the social reform that began in the nineteenth century. Trains also offered travel that was affordable to all but the very poorest, altering the way that the economic classes interacted and changing the natural barriers in Victorian British society.

As a general rule, historians find it difficult to isolate events in history and argue their impact upon society, when they are so well woven into the continuous tapestry of life. However, it is perhaps because of how embedded steam railways are in the development of the modern world that allows us to say they changed the world. Our lives right now are a direct result of the innovators, visionaries, designers, workers and daily users that created and advanced the steam railways. Had that development not have happened as it did, we would be living in a very different society today. Arguably, many of the problems we face today are an indirect consequence of economic, social and political developments in the nineteenth century, but so too are the solutions. Thanks to the introduction of the railways, we may have lost some sense of British *regionality*, but we can offset that against a sense of British unity.

It is impossible to contain the entire story of the railways in only one volume.

> **"TRAINS CUT THROUGH IMPOVERISHED URBAN ENVIRONMENTS AND GAVE MANY THEIR FIRST TASTE OF HOW THE OTHER HALF LIVED."**

The railways gave many people an insight into the horror of urban slum dwellings for the first time. This is Wentworth Street, Whitechapel, in Victorian London, as depicted in an engraving by Gustave Doré, 1872.

There are countless little anecdotes and backstories that deserve coverage but which would fill many hundreds of pages beyond those contained in this book. For example, did you know that when the *Flying Scotsman* was running low on supplies or had an onboard emergency, the crew would write a note, insert it into a potato and throw it at a signal box as the train passed by? They did this because, at the time, there was no other way to contact or alert the outside world. However, once the signalman had received the flying potato with its important missive, he could telegraph ahead to ensure that the speeding train's problem could be addressed further down the line.

Stories like this one and the many nuances of historic railway travel are infinite and most of them lost in time. However, this book is our attempt to go a little deeper than we can on a television screen, to examine a little more closely the detailed history of the railways. To the best of our knowledge the contents are accurate, but we apologise for any mistakes. We hope you enjoy reading about how the railways of Britain changed our lives forever.

Peter, Alex and Ruth welcome you to this book accompanying their television series and hope you will enjoy reading about the establishment of Britain's steam railways.

It was heavy industry that spawned the railways and the railways that were then to drive the expansion of heavy industry. The two went hand-in-hand, mutually supportive and entirely co-dependent throughout much of the nineteenth and twentieth centuries.

The Ffestiniog railway in the heart of Wales is the world's oldest surviving narrow gauge railway, dating back to 1832. It is thirteen and a half miles long and runs between Ffestiniog and Porthmadog, through some of the most dramatic and beautiful of Britain's countryside. The railway was built in order to transport slate from the quarry to the docks, bypassing a long overland route by packhorse, cart and river boat. Small manageable wagons could thence be loaded right at the quarry mouth and moved smoothly, without any slate-damaging jolts and knocks down to the harbour quayside, within a couple of hours. It was a vast improvement over the old system. Even a narrow gauge wagon could carry a much bigger load than a packhorse, and it cut out entirely the need to then unload the slate from those horses and reload it into small, flat-bottomed riverboats. These then had to be sailed downstream with the tide along the somewhat energetic but shallow river Dwryrd, only to need unloading again before the slate was transferred to the sea-going vessels. Just one year earlier, the tax upon the coastal transport of slate had been lifted – and the overland routes and imports had been significantly unburdened by this financial control – so the moment was ripe for the Welsh slate quarries to increase their production and share of the market. The owners of the Ffestiniog quarry, Samuel Holland and Henry Archer – the first a quarryman and the latter a Dublin businessman – decided that this was the moment to invest. What they decided to construct was a railway line of a type that they were familiar with, a tried and tested technology that had enhanced and expanded the businesses of several of their quarrying neighbours. Because, despite its status as the oldest surviving narrow gauge line, the Ffestiniog railway was by no means the first, even in the mountains of Wales, and it was entirely lacking in locomotives.

THE EARLIEST RAILWAYS

Railways existed long before steam locomotives and even before static steam engines. Indeed, the first recorded mention of a railed way for wagons in Britain can be dated to the very start of the seventeenth

century – in 1603, the same year that Elizabeth I died. Over the next two centuries, many remote sites from Northumberland to Snowdonia constructed flat or gently sloping track-ways with wooden guide rails, so that heavy loads could be moved easily around in a controlled manner using muscle power – either that of humans or horses. Mines and quarries were the major users of this transport system, as they were the businesses that had the heaviest and bulkiest of materials to move in volume. It was the weight of the loads that made a railed way so preferable to an open roadway. Rails provided a way of spreading the wagon's heavy load across the ground, rather than it being concentrated upon the couple of inches where the wheel met the road surface. Where road vehicles quickly churned up the mud and became stuck, railed wagons glided across. Rails also helped control the direction in which a wagon moved and kept it within a series of set locations. Mines and quarries were busy places that often featured many narrow passageways and restricted spaces, so this element of control and organization was extremely valuable.

As time went on, mine and quarry owners refined the systems that they used – improving wagon shapes, finding ways of making stable, well-drained trackways and, from around 1760, adding iron strips to the top of their wooden rails in order to prevent excessive wear. Fully iron rails arrived a generation later, cast in three- or four-foot long sections. It was this well-developed, muscle-powered railway that appeared upon the hills of Snowdonia in 1798, when the Ffestiniog's neighbour, the Penrhyn quarry, built its railway. Railways then were the servants of industry; they were shaped by its needs and they existed in places wherever industry needed them – often far from centres of population. However, at this time the railways were still very much a junior partner in the complex networks of waterways, sea routes and roads that joined up the trade of the British Isles.

SLATE

When the Ffestiniog railway was first built, it was constructed so that the two rails were 23½ inches apart (this distance between the rails is what is referred to by the word 'gauge'). Such a restricted gauge was chosen partly because a narrow gauge requires a much smaller path to be cut through tunnels and cuttings. It also uses less expensive, narrow bridges and fewer materials altogether. However, the narrow 23½-inch gauge was also chosen because this was the gauge of the rails that were already in use underground within the quarry.

The narrow gauge used for the Ffestiniog railway was inexpensive and designed to enable access to the darkest corners of mines and other inaccessible areas.

Ffestiniog slate was of the highest quality. It could be easily split and fashioned, was ideal for lightweight, supremely waterproof roofs and was also cheaper than most competing materials.

Some slate is quarried in an open-cast fashion, but the quarry at Ffestiniog is more akin to a conventional mine. The slate here is of a very high quality, allowing it to be split by hand into remarkably thin, consistent and structurally sound layers. In 1935, one Ffestiniog worker described how a single piece, only one inch thick, could be split into 26 layers, so that each slate would be a little less than a millimetre thick. Such thin layers were also fairly elastic and, crucially, they did not absorb water. This meant that slate from this deposit could be used to make superb roof tiles. They were very light due to their thinness, were able to cope with the slight warping of roof timbers and they did not become heavier when it rained. This meant that a roof covered in Welsh slate could be constructed from much lighter, thinner timbers than that of any other available material. The Ffestiniog slate shed water beautifully, too, meaning that roofs could be built with a far less steep pitch to them. Imagine the impact that all this had upon house building at the time. Indeed, you can see it around you to this day. The roofs of old cottages that were built to take thatch have a very steep pitch (around 70 per cent), even if the thatch itself is long gone. Think instead of the rows and rows of Victorian houses – the roofs are much shallower, rarely pitched at no more than a 45-degree angle, 30 degrees being much more common. The costs of building such a slate-roofed home with its smaller surface area and smaller, lighter timbers was substantially less than that of building a thatched home.

Due to an expanding population, the demand for cheap, yet properly watertight houses was high. The townscapes of Britain were utterly transformed as the slate industry blossomed. And it grew very largely because of the improved transport that the railways offered. While the output of the quarries had to be carried away by packhorse and small riverboat, there was little incentive to increase production – the quarry owners would simply not have been able to shift much more material. However, even without locomotive power, the railway could move exponentially more material, as well as moving it more quickly. Moreover, this new method of transport, whilst requiring an initially large capital outlay, was much cheaper to run. In many ways, the slate industry is simultaneously an example of an industry with a latent market waiting to be filled as well as one bursting with resources ready to

> "THE SLATE HERE IS OF A **VERY HIGH QUALITY,** ALLOWING IT TO BE SPLIT BY HAND INTO THIN, CONSISTENT AND SOUND LAYERS."

be exploited. Transport was the bottleneck. The railway opened up the flow, and money and people poured in.

In 1808, the entire parish of Ffestiniog was home to 732 people; by 1880, that figure had risen to 11,274.

During the nineteenth century, the only real competition for slate as a roofing material was tiles. However, in the 1830s these were still heavier than slate and also expensively hand produced. Of course, slate also required a good deal of handwork, from extraction to shaping – but it was still cheaper to produce. The quarrymen worked in small gangs of between four and eight men and their wages were determined by the finished output of the gang. About half the members of the gang would be 'rock men', who cut the slate out of the ground. The others would be equally divided between 'splitters' and 'dressers', who shaped the rock into slates. Independently of these gangs, 'bad rock men' were employed to remove other rock that was impeding progress and 'rubbish men' to remove the waste rock. By 1860, sawing, planing and dressing machines assisted in dividing up the large rough blocks into more manageable pieces for the splitters to work with, and helped trim the edges into regular, standardized rectangles. Rather than reducing the amount of work as such, mechanization allowed for faster processing, which in turn brought costs and prices down. All these factors made slate even more competitive as a product compared with its main alternative, tile.

The Ffestiniog railway line is a remarkable feat of engineering. With no motive power, the loaded wagons were intended simply to run down to the quay under the force of gravity. That meant that the gradient of the line had to be a steady one-in-eighty. If the railway became steeper, the trucks might speed up and run themselves off the rails at the bends;

Victorian quarrymen were a hardy breed, who largely fashioned slate by hand, before the mechanistic advances of the mid- to late nineteenth century.

OPPOSITE: These days the Ffestiniog railway no longer transports slate – only passengers. However, its proud heritage lives on.

OVERLEAF: Historian Ruth Goodman aboard the Ffestiniog railway steam train Prince.

SLATE MINING

Widely known as 'blue gold', the slate extracted from Welsh mines has been used to cover roofs across the globe. Welsh slate mining was an industry that expanded with the railways. It began with simple horse-drawn railways that took the slate from the mine to the ports and ended with an extensive rail network that could move vast quantities of heavy loads across the entire country.

Prior to descending into the mine, we looked at the exposed stratigraphy of the rocks around us. The band of slate was quite clear and went down into the ground at a 35-degree angle. We entered the mine, went down the trackway that would have once been used to haul up the slate, and found ourselves in a different world. The mine we were in was the second largest slate mine in Wales (the biggest was just across the road). Branching off a central circular passage were a number of caverns from which the slate was extracted. I was asked by our television sound engineer, 'why are you whispering?', and the only answer I could give was that the mine reminded me of a cathedral.

Families which lived near the Welsh slate mines often worked together in gangs and were paid according to the amount of usable slate that they produced. Once you were assigned a plot, as a miner you had to see it through until the slate was exhausted. This could easily take up to 30 years. As a rule of thumb, of all the material extracted from the ground, only ten per cent was usable as roof tiles. The rest was cast onto giant heaps adjacent to the railway near the entrance of the mine. This has completely changed the surrounding landscape, effectively creating new hills.

Slate is a sedimentary rock formed in layers that are easily visible to the naked eye. To mine it, holes were drilled by hand, perpendicular to the grain. On a new face of slate, before a platform was created upon which the miners could work, the first holes had to be drilled. To do this the miners used a chain wrapped around one of their legs, which supported their weight.

Slate is a relatively soft rock, so the drill that makes a hole which can be filled with powder and a fuse to blast a new face is simply an iron rod with a bulbous section that is heavy near to one end. The short end of the rod is used to start the hole and the long end to finish it. The drill is simply moved up and down by hand and the weight pulverizes the rock below to dust.

We were in the mine with electric lights and modern access routes. When the mine was fully operational in the nineteenth century, each cavern may have been lit by just one candle. The miners covered their own expenses, so burning lots of candles would impact on profit. The work was repetitive, often dangerous – especially when blasting – and the men spent much of their time chained to rocks in the half-light. In some instances, it is easy to imagine these conditions breaking the spirits of the miners, but in Wales it was quite the opposite. Poetry, song and political ideology were all penned in the mines. Lunch was taken in a *caban* (Welsh for cabin) built out of discarded slate in the mine area that the men were working. It was here that many discussions took place – and they were often minuted, so some records of their contents still survive to this day. Competitions with miners from other caverns also took place, often based on song or poetry.

However, it was above on the surface where the real competition was arguably happening. The slate taken up there had to be cut down to size in order to make the roof tiles. Tiles ranged in sizes and had names such as 'king' (largest), 'empress', 'princess' or 'lady', according to their dimensions. The skill of the cutter and the speed at which he worked would directly impact upon the usable product produced. The rock had to be sawn, split and trimmed – and slate dust is not kind to the lungs....

if the line flattened out, there was the danger of the wagons slowing to a standstill. Only the very last portion of the line was level, where the momentum of the loaded wagons was enough to allow them to run on for a distance before gently stopping just before the quayside. The surveying and construction skills involved in the building of the line can still be seen and appreciated today, as the line snakes its way around the hillside over embankments and through cuttings, following the contours of the landscape. Such skills had been honed in building the canals, and by the mid-nineteenth century they were the stock in trade of a large body of professional men and skilled labourers.

STEAM

However, we must not forget steam. That, too, has a long and convoluted history. Claims that such and such was 'the man who invented the steam engine' tend to obscure the fact that all great people stand upon the shoulders of giants. Look closer, and what you see is a long journey of ideas, experiments, refinements and improvements, with the baton of progress moving from one hand to another, and advancements often dependent on other tangential developments. Amongst all the great visionaries and engineers involved in the story of steam engines, one of the greatest was James Watt. Using huge skill, he applied new scientific thinking from the academic world and combined it with what he discovered by analyzing the working model of another man's engine. This statement, of course, does not take anything away from Watt's genius or his astonishingly hard work. But steam engines did not simply pop into existence one night after somebody watched a kettle boiling…

The young James Watt was a clever lad who did not really fit within the usual schooling system of his day, having no head for Latin or Greek; however, he did have both a good feel for numbers (his grandfather had set up a school of mathematics) and for practical matters. Watt's father was a gifted maker of precision instruments who gave his son a set of small tools as a present. As a child, James was reported as enjoying nothing more than taking his toys apart and putting them back together, often in different combinations. One of his father's workmen even remarked that he thought 'Jamie' would have 'fortune at his fingers' ends'. It was years later, when he was working for the professors of the University in Glasgow producing the

> "AS A CHILD, JAMES WAS REPORTED AS ENJOYING NOTHING MORE THAN TAKING HIS TOYS APART AND PUTTING THEM BACK TOGETHER."

instruments and apparatus that they required for teaching and research – as well as making musical instruments – that James Watt's researches into steam power began. Ideas had been discussed and models made from the latter part of the seventeenth century onwards, and the first commercial steam-powered engine had emerged back in 1698, when Thomas Savery produced his 'Fire Engine'. This machine could pull water vertically upwards for a distance of forty feet, earning it the nickname, 'the miner's friend'. It addressed a newly urgent problem. The mines of southern England were reaching greater depths and experiencing severe flooding problems. Traditional methods of pumping out all this water using horse or water power were proving inadequate, both systems being unable to move sufficient amounts of water from such depths. In practice, Savery's engines were prone to exploding, with catastrophic and often fatal consequences, but it was clear to everyone within the mining and engineering community that steam power was the way forward. After several people had made improvements to Savery's invention, the next major leap came in 1712, when Thomas Newcomen devised a beam engine that could drive a piston. The five horsepower that Newcomen's engine could produce more than doubled the power of the Savery engine, and this machine proved to be altogether a much safer beast. It would be this engine that transformed mining capabilities across the country and which so intrigued and inspired James Watt around fifty years later.

In the late eighteenth century, Glasgow University was a forward-looking institution, interested in and supportive of many different kinds of scientific investigation. So perhaps it comes as no surprise that it should have owned a working model of a Newcomen engine. However, for 'working', read 'broken'… Attempts to repair the model in London appeared to be going nowhere, so the engine was returned to Glasgow and was handed over to James Watt. The model revealed several shortcomings to Watt and sent him off on a furious search through the scientific literature of the day. However, since much of that literature was not in the English language, he had first to learn French, Italian and German before he could decipher a lot of key information. Watt might well have disliked business – *I would rather face a loaded cannon than settle an account or make a bargain* – and had indeed been involved in several business failures, but he was nonetheless an incredibly inventive and driven man who was unafraid of

> **"WHEN PEOPLE SAY 'JAMES WATT INVENTED THE STEAM ENGINE', THEY MEAN HE WAS THE FIRST TO COME UP WITH THE IDEA OF CONDENSING STEAM."**

James Watt improved Thomas Newcomen's basic design in 1769, with a more efficient engine featuring a cylinder that stayed hot.

hard intellectual as well as physical work. By several accounts, James Watt was also a pleasant man to be around; for example, his workshop at the university became a popular place for academics, engineers and others to gather and socialize. Combining all he had learnt from the scientific papers and from the model of Newcomen's engine, Watt began to investigate the theory of 'latent heat'. At this time, he discovered that another man at the university, Professor Robert Black, had already come up with the theory and had even been teaching it for several years. Some lesser men might have given up at that point, but Watt was not a man of petty jealousies; neither was Robert Black, and so the pair teamed up.

When people say '*James Watt invented the steam engine*', what they mean is that he was the first to come up with the idea of condensing the steam in a separate chamber. Born out of his hard-won understanding of latent heat, he could see that Newcomen's engine lost most of its power re-heating the cylinder after each stroke. Newcomen's piston was driven when hot steam pushed in one direction, a spray of cold water cooled the steam, and the piston was drawn back by the resultant

vacuum. However, each cooling cycle cooled not only the steam but the cylinder, too. Watt realized that the now cool cylinder was drawing much of the potential energy of the steam, simply to reheat it on every stroke, making Newcomen's engine supremely inefficient. Having identified and analysed the scientific problem, Watt then had to find a way of solving it mechanically. Many of his early attempts were dogged by the difficulty of getting truly precision parts made. The theory and designs were basically right in principle, but the skill levels of many of the workmen he had to rely on sometimes let him down.

It would take many years of hard slog, further technical insight and invention to sort out the technical difficulties of full-scale production. Watt's major backer and business partner during this period was Joe Roebuck, who owned the Carron colliery and had the foresight to see that steam-powered engines were the way forward. However, the development of Watt's engine took more time and money than Joe Roebuck's business could support. Consequently, Watt had to abandon full-time developmental work and work as a surveyor – a job that he

James Watt was a powerful innovator, whose great expertise lay in analyzing and adapting the technical ideas and developments of other engineers.

hated – and Joe Roebuck, faced additionally with a small economic downturn, went bankrupt. That might well have been that – and James Watt could well have remained a footnote in history – if not for another example of different skills, ideas and histories coming together at the optimum moment.

Once he became bankrupt, Joe Roebuck's share in Watt's steam engine was bought out by one Matthew Boulton. Boulton was not an engineer, but rather a businessman – perhaps the first great businessman, a man who could be said to have invented the production line. He ran one of the largest factories in the world at Soho in Birmingham, and was a genius at marketing, networking and financial control. He was also hugely rich. With money, and the efforts of plenty of skilled (and more disciplined) workers and customers organized by Boulton, the first of Watt's rotary motion ten horsepower pressurized steam engines went into production in 1781. Steam power was no longer largely confined to pumping water out of mines – Boulton and Watt's engines, capable of providing a steady powered spinning motion, could be turned to a vast array of industrial processes. From hereon in, steam began to revolutionize a host of different businesses. It was Boulton rather than Watt who had seen the importance of rotary motion and how it could be successfully employed.

LOCOMOTIVES

Let us return to the Ffestiniog railway by way of the early steam engines, *Puffing Billy* and *The Rocket*. In 1832, as they launched their railway building project, Holland and Archer could conceivably have chosen to employ steam power, either from a static engine that could haul wagons up and down small inclines on the end of a rope or chain, or from a true steam locomotive. However, neither option would have seemed to be a particularly attractive proposition at that precise moment. The slate business enjoyed the benefit of only needing to transport their heavy wares down from the mountainside to the docks, so that exclusively empty, lighter wagons needed to make the journey back up. Consequently, a static engine designed to haul wagons back up inclines was unnecessary, so long as the wagons could be made light enough for a horse to do the job. As for a steam locomotive – well, in 1832 there was no narrow-gauge engine available that was strong enough to perform the role.

On 29 October 1804 at Pen-y-darren ironworks, Merthyr Tydfil, a self-propelled steam engine made its way along the iron railway towards

OVERLEAF: **Presenters Ruth Goodman, Alex Langlands and Peter Ginn on the Ffestiniog railway in north Wales.**

Richard Trevithick (1771–1833) was a Cornish inventor and mining engineer. His work built on that achieved by Watt and advanced the new science of steam locomotion.

Abercynon. The anonymous locomotive had been built by Richard Trevithick, who was well established as a steam engineer and had worked out a method of using pressurized steam that obviated the need for Watt's separate condenser. Trevithick adopted this approach, as he did not want to have to pay a licence fee for the use of Watt's patented device. Trevithick had experimented two years previously at Pen-y-darren, with the support of the owner and the assistance of Rees Jones, who was an employee of the ironworks. However, the 1804 run does not appear to have been a serious attempt to launch steam locomotion, but rather was staged to win a bet. A large crowd gathered to see the locomotive pull five wagons with ten tons of coal and seventy men the full nine and three quarter miles at walking pace. The bet was won, but the heavy engine broke the iron-topped wooden rails and was immediately retired from action. However, with so many people watching and with such an important name as Trevithick involved, it was not long before many other engineers began experimenting with locomotives.

The *Puffing Billy* locomotive was made in 1813 under William Hedley's patent No. 3666 for the Wylam colliery.

Puffing Billy is the oldest surviving locomotive in the world. It began work in 1814 at the Wylam colliery near Newcastle upon Tyne, hauling wagonloads of coal from the mine to Staithes landing quay on the river Tyne. The engine carried on doing this until 1862. Like the railways themselves, locomotives were designed for industry. Of course, the investment in building these still quite experimental engines was large, but so too were the potential profits. Transport costs contributed very substantially to the price of a commodity as heavy as coal. Just as slate had a ready and waiting market at the beginning of the nineteenth

A painting of a British coal mine pit head in 1820. Note the combined use of equine power, manpower and the great new innovation – steam.

OPPOSITE: A gigantic heap of coal at a modern coal-powered power station in Helsinki, Finland. It is the sheer volume of coal required for energy that has driven so much haulage technology over the decades.

century, so too did coal. The steam engines built by James Watt, Richard Trevithick and others were dotted around numerous mines and quarries, mills and foundries – and all ran on coal. Meanwhile, domestic demand for coal was also growing, as towns and cities with soaring populations found themselves outstripping the local supply of firewood. The Wylam colliery owner realized that if he could cut his transport costs and therefore his prices, he would have no trouble selling much larger volumes of coal. Like many of his competitors, he already owned an iron-topped wooden railway with wagons hauled by horses, but he could see the possibilities in the new technology and was willing to invest.

Initially, Wylam colliery also had trouble with the weight of the engine (eight tons), which damaged rails, but they persevered. *Puffing Billy* was one of three engines that ran on the line and was designed by a team that included the engineer Thomas Hedley, the engineman Jonathan Forster, the blacksmith Timothy Hackworth and the colliery owner Christopher Blackett. Such collaboration between men of very

DIFFERENT TYPES OF COAL

Not all coal is the same. Stand in the yards of any of the preserved railways or at any steam fair in the country and you will hear grumbling about 'the wrong sort' of coal. Every coal deposit has a different chemical composition that affects how much energy it releases when burnt, how quickly and hotly it burns, and how much tar and smoke it produces in the process.

Steam engines require the very best stuff – the clean-burning coals that will not coat the firebox and boiler tubes with tar. They also need coal that is highly calorific, giving the engines the energy they need to work, and they need it to have a very low water content. From the very beginning of the era of steam railways, south Wales had a reputation for producing top quality 'steam coal' – particularly the area around Merthyr Tydfil. Domestic fires do not have quite the same need for high-end anthracite type coals; they might burn better using good coal, but they can work on much cheaper, dirtier, wetter and less calorific types. The cheapest varieties of coal are the brown coals that are halfway between peat and anthracite, but even the best 'house coals' are cheaper and of lower quality than 'steam coal'.

Consequently, throughout the days of steam travel, there was a thriving cross-country trade in different types of coal. It was perfectly common for a colliery that produced mainly domestic coal to have to bring in steam coal in order to fire its pumping engines and locomotives.

different social backgrounds and classes is a real feature of the early history of the railways. They were dealing with cutting-edge technology and there was no time for vested interests to be indulged. Expertise, intelligence and enthusiasm were welcome wherever they were found (although, of course, not from women…).

Many of the intervening locomotives between Trevithick's anonymous engine and *Puffing Billy* moved on a form of rack and pinion system in order to maintain traction. However, the Wylam colliery engines had smooth wheels and ran upon a smooth track. Their success as working vehicles proved once and for all that on gentle inclines iron wheels upon iron track provided plenty of grip – although in slippery conditions, a little sand sprinkled onto the tracks every now and again could be helpful. Moving at what now seems a very stately five miles per hour, *Puffing Billy* made quite a visual impact. Upon a casual glance, the engine presents a rather confused picture, with rods, beams and shafts sticking up and moving about in several directions at once. There is certainly no indication of streamlining, or much in the way of facilities for the crew. In fact, *Puffing Billy* looks much more like a slightly flimsy static engine mounted upon an astonishingly sturdy cart with a chimney bolted on the front. You can even see large cog-wheels beneath the cart bed. Behind it ran another little wagon full of coal, and out in front of the engine ran a second one, carrying a large barrel full of water. Unsurprisingly,

The Rainhill Trials, October 1829. These were conducted to find a locomotive for the world's first fully steam-hauled railway – the Liverpool and Manchester – which opened the following year.

considering the rather precarious-looking arrangement of rods and beams, the engine wobbles and judders rather a lot when it is in motion. Many people think that the phrase '*to run like Billy-o*' was inspired by *Puffing Billy*. There is no doubt that in 1814 it was considered to be a fast machine – and to this day all that shaking about still gives a sense of bustle.

The *Rocket* is still the most famous steam engine in the world. Built by the father and son team George and Robert Stephenson, it set the world speed record in 1829 at the Rainhill Trials, when it reached 36 miles per hour. These speeds seem so slow now to us, almost two hundred years later. However, in 1829 no one on earth had ever travelled

The *Rocket* was designed
by Robert Stephenson
and built at his Forth
Street works in
Newcastle-upon-Tyne in
1829. Although not the
first steam locomotive,
essentially it was the
template for most other
steam engines for the
next 150 years.

TRAVELLING ON THE LIVERPOO

faster than a horse could gallop – and most people had never even owned a horse to gallop upon. Only fifteen years previously, *Puffing Billy* had been considered speedy at just five miles per hour, and the Stephensons themselves were surprised at *Rocket*'s performance. It was also a considerably better-looking machine than poor old *Puffing Billy*. Much of the confusion of beams, rods and shafts had gone – instead, this engine looked sleek and punchy. The Stephensons had created something quite revolutionary, mixing together their own unique vision with everything they had learned from a host of other engineers. In part, the Stephensons' success stemmed from their understanding that this engine needed to do something quite different from all those that had gone before – namely, carry passengers. Of course, many people had ridden in wagons pulled by steam engines before on an ad hoc basis, but passengers and their speedy transit were the challenge that the Liverpool and Manchester railway had set. Their business model did not involve moving coal or slate from mine to dock: it involved the linking of two cities, the Liverpool and Manchester of their name. Yes, they expected

The Liverpool and Manchester Railway, pictured in 1831, several months after its inauguration. This was the world's first passenger railway service.

MANCHESTER RAILWAY. 1831.

on the top of the front carriage and directed the Engine Driver, whilst the Royal Mail Man guarded the Mail box in the rear

...y comparable in the History of Science to that grand triumphal march-for such it was-with which the Liverpool & Manchester Railway was opened

there to be freight on board the trains, but they were also looking for passenger traffic. The company set up the competition to decide who would get the contract to build the new locomotives for their railway. The rules were clear. Firstly, there was a weight restriction to prevent damage to the rails, which as we have seen, was a recurrent problem at this time. The passengers were to be carried a full sixty miles. This, too, was a challenge. Early engines such as *Puffing Billy* were designed for travelling quite short distances, averaging around fifteen miles in one stretch, and needed to stop and refill with water in between runs. However, the directors of the Liverpool and Manchester railway company were looking for reliability and speed, so that they could run regular services.

Probably most of the credit for designing the *Rocket* deserves to go to the younger of the two Stephensons, Robert. His father, George,

"MUCH OF THE **CONFUSION OF BEAMS**, RODS AND SHAFTS HAD GONE – INSTEAD, THIS ENGINE LOOKED **SLEEK AND PUNCHY.**"

COOKING WITH COAL

As someone who has a lot of practical experience of cooking upon a variety of both wood and coal fires, I can honestly say that I think wood is very much my preferred fuel. Wood is tremendously controllable. Of course, you need skill to get the best out of it, but if you know what you are doing it is possible to control wood fires with more accuracy than can be achieved using any modern appliance. Unlike electric plates or halogen hobs, wood fires respond instantly – and they also add a distinctive flavour to food. On the other hand, coal is slow to heat up and cool down, the merest hint of its smoke gives the food an unpleasant taste, and it is filthy to work with. Wood ash is easy to clean up, there is usually very little of it and it leaves no stains. In the case of coal, however, there is always lots of ash and the black smuts that fall like snowflakes leave greasy, staining marks on everything in the vicinity.

In the nineteenth century, when household after household converted to coal fires, they did not do so because it was a better fuel. Rather, they made the change because it was cheaper. However, coal must be substantially cheaper before people are induced into making such a change, not just because of its general inferiority, but because of the costs of the conversion required for burning it. A wood fire simply requires a space, and hopefully a chimney and some round-bottomed pans on legs. Of course, the big kitchens of Victorian grand establishments were equipped with far more equipment than that – the burning brands of wood were held upon brandreths or trivets, and spit dogs were used to hold spits in front of them. Many big kitchens had a sort of crane fixed into the chimney from which a pot could be suspended, and some had mechanical devices for turning their spits. However, within the commoner's cottage you could if necessary dispense with all that expensive ironware – even your cooking pots might be just inexpensive earthenware, if necessary.

Put a pile of coal on the floor in the hearth and you will soon discover how difficult it is to cook upon. It needs far more draught than wood in order to burn at all, so as an absolute minimum you will need an iron basket in which to put your coal, so that the air can get to it properly. The next thing you will discover is that the pots and pans you use over your wooden fire will not work so well over coal. The earthenware variety will quickly succumb to heat shock, and all those round-bottomed metal pots are no longer efficient over the varying, different-shaped flames. Therefore, if you want to cook over a coal fire, you will have to invest in a new set of metal pans.

As the nineteenth century progressed, coal did become markedly cheaper and wood became ever more difficult to source and purchase. As coal became less expensive, so more people converted their fireplaces. Similarly, as demand for coal rose, the collieries became more willing to invest in railways, and as railways spread, the coal became progressively cheaper to transport and buy. It was a powerful and irresistible cycle of supply and demand.

ABOVE AND LEFT: An archetypal Victorian kitchen, shown together with an array of contemporary utensils. This is actually the perfectly preserved kitchen at Lanhydrock House in Cornwall. Copper pots and pans hang from the wall above the cooking range, which would have been fired by coal.

LIVERPOOL, OCTOBER 5, 1829.

A LIST OF THE ENGINES

Entered to contend at RAINHILL, on the 6th of OCTOBER instant,

FOR

THE PREMIUM OF £500,

OFFERED BY

The Directors of the Liverpool and Manchester Rail-road,

FOR THE

BEST LOCOMOTIVE POWER.

No. 1.—Messrs. Braithwaite and Erickson, of London; "The Novelty;"
     Copper and Blue; weight 2T. 15CWT.

2.—Mr. Ackworth, of Darlington; "The Sans Pareil;" Green, Yellow,
     and Black; weight 4T. 8CWT. 2Q.

3.—Mr. Robert Stephenson, Newcastle-upon-Tyne; "The Rocket;"
     Yellow and Black, White Chimney; weight 4T. 3CWT.

4.—Mr. Brandreth, of Liverpool; "The Cycloped;" weight ~~3 T.~~; *3 Tons*
     worked by a Horse.

5.—Mr. Burstall, Edinburgh; "The Perseverance;" Red Wheels;
     weight 2T. 17CWT.

The Engines to be ready at Ten o'Clock on Tuesday Morning. The
Running Ground will be on the Manchester side of the Rainhill Bridge.

The Load attached to each Engine will be three times the weight of the
Engine.

No Person, except the Directors and Engineers will be permitted to
enter or cross the Rail-road.

J. U. RASTRICK, Esq., Stourbridge, C.E. ⎫
NICHOLAS WOOD, Esq., Killingworth, C.E. ⎬ Judges.
JOHN KENNEDY, Esq., Manchester, ⎭

"THE GREAT DAY ARRIVED. TEN LOCOMOTIVES HAD BEEN ENTERED INTO THE RACE AND VAST CROWDS GATHERED. THE PRESS WERE THERE IN NUMBERS."

PREVIOUS PAGES: The Foxfield Railway is a preserved standard gauge line located south east of Stoke-on-Trent. The line was built in 1893 to serve the colliery at Dilhorne on the Cheadle coalfield. It joined the North Staffordshire Railway line near Blythe Bridge in the eighteenth and early nineteenth centuries.

OPPOSITE: Page 37 from the notebook belonging to John Urpeth Rastrick (1780–1856), used to record details of the Rainhill locomotive trials in 1829. Rastrick was one of the judges.

was busy elsewhere designing and supervising the building of the Liverpool and Manchester railway line, although the two kept in close touch. There were a great deal of technical improvements incorporated within *Rocket*, but probably the most important and the one to have the longest-term impact was the multi-tube boiler. The older engines worked by wrapping a large canister full of water around the chimney of a firebox. The hot smoke and air from the fire travelled along the chimney and heated the water as it passed through the horizontal section within the canister of water (the boiler) and then escaped vertically up the chimney at the far end. The rocket had not one but 25 parallel tubes that carried the hot gases through the boiler full of water. With so much more surface area contact between the hot tubes and the water, far more of the energy could be transferred. Put simply, 25 small hot pokers plunged into a bucket of water will heat that water very much more quickly than one large hot poker. When the much cooler gases reached the end of the boiler, they were allowed to come together again to escape up the chimney, aided by a shot of steam. This 'blast pipe' system fed a small stream of exhaust steam into the base of the vertical chimney, creating a vacuum that in turn created a fierce 'draw'. In addition, the *Rocket* also made use of the radiant heat of the firebox by giving it a double skin and passing water through between the two layers. The *Rocket* was designed to be light and fast, but not particularly strong. Passengers in their carriages are a much lighter load than wagons of coal or slate, and *Rocket* was intended from the outset to pull no more than three times its own weight.

The great day arrived. Ten locomotives had been entered into the race and vast crowds gathered. The great and the influential had all been invited, the press were there in numbers from all over the world – with a particularly large contingent from the United States. Five of the engines never made it to Rainhill, problems with design, manufacturing and reliability forcing them to withdraw. Two more arrived but had to withdraw on the day. Just three engines were still in the running. Fireboxes were lit and steam began to build.

It is hard to overplay the public interest that this event generated. This was an arena displaying the absolute white heat of the technology of the time. All the various small-scale lines, the experiments and the stuttering commercial successes of the last few decades had shown that

GEORGE STEPHENSON (1781–1848)

George Stephenson was world-famous in his lifetime and has not been forgotten since. His father worked at the Wylam colliery near Newcastle upon Tyne, shovelling coal into the firebox of the static pumping engine, and the family lived alongside the wooden railway. Thus, rail and steam entered George's life, almost from the first. However, his was a family with few of the advantages that usually offer hopes of success. Neither of his parents could read or write and George, like so many children in the last years of the eighteenth century, was working out in the fields from the age of six or seven. School would have cost money that his family simply did not have. By the age of ten, George was driving the horse-drawn, coal-filled wagons along the wooden railed way. Life began to change when he moved from tending horses to following in his father's footsteps and instead began tending steam engines.

As a 17-year-old engineman, George had a few pennies to spare, and these he chose to spend upon an education, attending night school after a long day at the pit. Within the year, George had learnt to read and write and handle basic arithmetic. Such determination and drive were to be lifelong traits. Over the next few years, George Stephenson moved around the local pits, working in one menial capacity or another upon the static engines. Finally, in 1811 at High Pit Killington, he got a chance to shine when he fixed a broken-down engine and was promoted to the position of engineer. This was a huge social leap, one that would not have been possible if he had remained illiterate, and still one that probably raised a few eyebrows in the class-conscious days of the early nineteenth century. Immersed in steam technology, intimately familiar with railed ways, ambitious and intelligent, George was hearing regular reports of the experiments taking place with locomotives, the hot topic of the day in colliery circles. It was almost inevitable that he would become a builder of steam engines. His first working example Blucher was ready in 1814. He had modelled it upon one built by Matthew Murray that was working nearby, but he must also have seen Puffing Billy, which entered service that year upon the Wylam colliery railway, just outside his childhood home.

In 1819, George moved on from engine building to the construction of entire railways. His first was an eight-mile section of track for Hetton colliery that ran entirely upon mechanical power – a world first – with gravity providing downhill motion and locomotives working on the level and slight upward inclines. There was no holding Stephenson back now. Ten years later, the opening of the Stockton and Darlington Railway took place. This seminal event is often cited as the dawn of modern railways. It was one of George Stephenson's engineering projects. In a whirlwind of activity, he persuaded investors to put up money, surveyed the route, designed cuttings and embankments, organized and supervised the labour, designed and built the engines, set up a new dedicated engine building company to do so (the first ever) and ran a PR campaign. As far as George was concerned, the days when railways were only of interest to those involved in mining and quarrying were over. His vision was for railways that moved everything and everyone.

'Railways will come to supersede almost all other methods of conveyance in this country, when mail coaches will go by railway, and railroads will become the Great Highway for the King and all his subjects. The time is coming when it will be cheaper for a working man to travel on a railway than to walk on foot. I know that there are great and almost insurmountable difficulties that will have to be encountered; but what I have said will come to pass as sure as we live.'

(George Stephenson, 1825)

Well before the Stockton and Darlington opened, Stephenson was already working on the Liverpool and Manchester railway – a line that would focus on moving people rather than coal.

From the moment that the *Rocket* reached its top speed of 36 miles per hour at the Rainhill Trials in 1829, George, and increasingly his son Robert, were at the very heart of an explosion in British railways. As enthusiasm boiled over and line after line was developed and promoted across the whole country, everyone wanted the father and son team of the Stephensons on board.

THE HUSKISSON INCIDENT

'You probably have by this time heard and read accounts of the opening of the railroad, and the fearful accident which occurred at it, for the papers are full of nothing else.... The engine had stopped to take in a supply of water, and several of the gentlemen in the directors' carriage had jumped out to look about them. Lord W.-, Count Batthyany, Count Matuscenitz, and Mr Huskisson among the rest were standing talking in the middle of the road, when an engine on the other line, which was parading up and down merely to show its speed, was seen coming down upon them like lightning. The most active of those in peril sprang back into their seats: Lord W.- saved his life only by rushing behind the Duke's carriage, and Count Matuscenitz had but just leaped into it, with the engine all but touching his heels as he did so; while poor Mr Huskisson, less active from the effects of age and ill health, bewildered, too, by the frantic cries of 'Stop the engine! Clear the track!' that resounded on all sides, completely lost his head, looked helplessly to the right and left, and was instantly prostrated by the fatal machine, which dashed like a thunderbolt upon him'.

(Fanny Kemble, 1830)

Engraved by J. Cochran, from an Original Picture painted for John Gladstone Esq. of Seaforth House, near Liverpool, by John Graham, Esq. of Edinburgh, three months previous to Mr Huskisson's death.

THE RIGHT HON^{BLE} WILLIAM HUSKISSON.

W Huskisson.

FISHER, SON & Co LONDON, 1836.

This tragic accident occurred during the opening ceremony of the Liverpool and Manchester Railway in 1830, the line built by George Stephenson and the line that the *Rocket* was built to run on. Hugh crowds had gathered to watch and a host of important people invited. Mr Huskisson was one of those VIPs. He was the MP for Liverpool, a man generally liked and admired. Should such an accident happen now to so prominent a person in the context of a new technology, it is hard to imagine that technology having any future at all. However, it is testament to the cheapness of life – even elite life – in the early nineteenth century, and to the enormous wave of excitement surrounding the new technology, that the whole incident passed with barely a blip. Certainly, the subsequent fortunes of the Liverpool and Manchester railway and other railway schemes were completely unaffected by the incident.

steam locomotives running on iron railways were the future. There might well still be technical difficulties, but it was easy to see that in time these would be ironed

> **"ROCKET STEAMED AHEAD ALMOST FROM THE FIRST AND GEORGE STEPHENSON BECAME AN OVERNIGHT INTERNATIONAL CELEBRITY."**

out, and that a new, connected world was just around the corner.

Rocket steamed ahead almost from the first and George Stephenson became an overnight international celebrity.

IRON INDUSTRY

It was not only locomotives that were developing quickly. Just as railways were closely tied to the needs and fortunes of the mining industries, so too were they entwined with the iron industry. Good quality iron, in quantity at affordable prices, was essential for anyone building locomotives or iron railways. The railways had been servants of the iron industry, moving coal and ore in the days of horsepower, and they continued in that role in the days of steam. However, they also sparked an international demand for the products of that industry, most directly and immediately a demand for rails.

The biggest name in this connection is Dowlais, an iron foundry that was already at the leading edge of innovation. In 1815, it was the largest producer of wrought iron in the world. Cast iron taken direct from the blast furnace is brittle, but wrought iron (iron that has been worked, driving out the excess carbon content and incorporating elements of slag within its crystalline structure), can bend and flex. The Dowlais Iron Company did not invent the wrought iron rails, but they did have the facilities, expertise and commercial muscle to produce them in quantity – vast quantity. They were able to take this British invention and sell it worldwide.

The rails were the result of the work of John Birkinshaw who worked, not for Dowlais, but for the Bedlington ironworks in Northumberland. When this company became involved in a local scheme for a railed wagon-way, Birkinshaw turned his attention to the problem of the rails themselves. Short lengths, three or four feet-long of solid cast iron, had taken over from the earlier system of wooden rails with an iron strip tacked on top, but problems with rails were endemic. They just kept breaking – particularly under the weight

OVERLEAF: **Presenter Peter Ginn stands on the footplate of an old steam train, dressed in period costume.**

of locomotives. Lengths of wrought iron produced by blacksmiths were being tried, but many people were sceptical, as wrought iron is notorious for its propensity to rust. Hearing of such experiments, Birkinshaw wrote to the agent of the Earl of Carlisle up at Tindal Fell, who owned both cast and wrought iron sections of track. The agent was unequivocal in his assessment: wrought iron was better. Tindal Fell had been using it for eight years and had not had to replace any wrought iron rails, whilst the cast iron sections had to be replaced '*almost daily*'. Nor did the wrought iron rails rust. The agent speculated that rust was kept at bay by the constant use and by '*condensation of the upper surface of the metal by the heavy weights rolled over it, which produces a hard compact coat, like that produced by cold hammering steel and copper plates.*' John Birkinshaw set about designing a method of producing such rails in long lengths and in large volume. He worked out how to shape the iron using a pair of shaped rollers and a '*powerful steam engine with*

Dowlais ironworks, Cardiff, at night. This painting is by the artist Lionel Walden and dates from the late 1890s.

Victorian ironworking in a foundry. This painting is the work of the French painter, Fernand Cormon (1845–1924), and was produced in 1893.

great velocity'. A red-hot iron bar was fed between the rollers and fifteen foot long lengths of rail emerged on the other side.

George Stephenson had patented his own improved rails, but after he had seen Birkinshaw's in action, he wrote to the promoters of the Stockton and Darlington railway: '*To tell you the truth, although it would put £500 in my pockets to specify my own patent rails, I cannot do so after the experiences I have had.*' Always open to new ideas and more interested in the success of the railway than in personal get-rich-quick schemes, Stephenson used Birkinshaw's rails and advised everyone else to do the same over the decades to come.

Production of those rails began with John Birkinshaw's employers, the Bedlington foundry, but it was to be the Dowlais firm that capitalized upon his invention to the greatest profit and benefit.

Back in 1783, Peter Onion (the brother-in-law of one of Dowlais' owners) had come up with and patented a method of 'puddling' pig

An extensive network of wrought iron rails was a pre-condition for creating the early railways. Fortunately, new technology was at hand to enable the mass production of iron that was required.

iron to turn it into wrought iron. Refinements were of course to follow, but this was the first time that it became possible to produce wrought iron in quantity. The old medieval small-scale bloomeries had produced wrought iron in small batches directly from the kiln. The new large-scale blast furnaces that are sometimes credited with kicking off the industrial revolution in the late eighteenth century produced much larger quantities, but it was pig iron that they output, not wrought iron. Pig iron was superb for casting, but if you needed wrought iron you were still dependent on the old bloomeries, until puddling came along. A combination of new industrial process, a good location and good business management made this firm in South Wales the centre of the international iron industry. Life in Merthyr Tydfil was changing fast. As a forward-looking business, Dowlais soon invested in one of Boulton and Watt's steam engines to drive the bellows on their blast furnace (the first one in Wales), and a second soon followed to power the new rolling mill that took the puddled wrought iron and rolled it out into bars. They were ready to expand their operations. As news trickled out of the success of Birkinshaw's wrought

> **"PIG IRON WAS SUPERB FOR CASTING, BUT IF YOU NEEDED WROUGHT IRON YOU WERE STILL DEPENDENT ON THE OLD BLOOMERIES."**

Coal ships moored at Cardiff docks in the late nineteenth century. The railways provided the missing link that enabled the coal to be transported directly to the water and the world.

iron rails, the Dowlais company could see the great potential that this new product had for them. Having cracked the problems of producing large quantities of wrought iron and got to grips with steam engines, they were perfectly placed to add one more rolling mill that could turn a useful material into a brand new finished product. They were keen to tender for any new railway business. According to Dowlais' records, they managed to sell rails to the Stockton and Darlington railway in 1829, although presumably most were actually made by the Bedlington Iron Foundry where Birkinshaw worked. They certainly supplied a large number the following year to the Liverpool and Manchester Railway. However, what made the real money were the offshore sales. By 1831, Dowlais were selling to the United States, providing all the rails for the Pennsylvania Railroad. Five years later, they had won contracts for the entire length of the Berlin and Leipzig line and that between St Petersburg and Pauloffsky. The Grand Duke Constantine of Russia himself came in person to witness the construction process. Twenty thousand tons of wrought iron rails left Dowlais that year along the newly built Taff Vale Railway down to Cardiff docks. Ten years later that tonnage had more than quadrupled, now produced by 18 great blast furnaces. It was

a vast enterprise, employing around one and half thousand adult men, nearly eight hundred adult women, about twelve hundred teenagers and another five hundred younger children. Meanwhile, as the people laboured, the ores to sustain these levels of production poured in from Whitehaven, Barrow, Cornwall, Northampton, the Forest of Dean and Spain, in addition to the native ores of Wales. Most of that ore, in a great industrial cycle, was brought in by rail.

The triumph of wrought iron rails lasted for a mere 35 years before they were ousted by steel. Just as a technical leap in iron production allowed wrought iron to move from small-scale to large-scale manufacture, the 'Bessemer process' made steel into a mass-market material. Steel rails promised to last four times longer and consequently cut the costs of track maintenance. Henry Bessemer patented his process in 1856 and Dowlais was the first firm to take out a licence to use it. However, it took them nine more years of experimentation and investment before the first steel rails rolled their way out of the factory on wagons of the Taff Valley Railway. Theirs were not in fact the first to be laid. That honour fell to a small section of railway line at Derby station, produced from the results of an abortive experiment with scrap metal and the Bessemer process by Robert Forester Mushet at the Ebbw Vale Ironworks. However, once again Dowlais was soon producing a huge volume of rails and the massive exports that went with this output.

Whether you analyse slate, coal or iron – or indeed a host of other industries – you cannot fail to see the symbiotic nature of their relationship with railways. Without the heavy industry, there would have been no track and no locomotives; but without first the track and later the locomotives, there would have been precious little industry. The two developed hand in hand, each taking the other up to the next level. Every advance for one sparked an advance for the other, throughout the nineteenth century.

CHAPTER 2

MOVING PEOPLE

As I sit on a train gliding through the countryside, moving more quickly than the cars I can see on a nearby motorway, I wonder to myself how the passenger experience has changed over the years. Trains are an established part of our lives. Whatever we may think about them as they go by, they are not new to us. However, when the railways were first built, the impact of trains on the surrounding countryside was immense.

The train I am travelling in is a thoroughly modern 'Pendolino', and there is an unbroken, if somewhat complex, lineage between this train and the very first passenger trains. The Pendolino is closely related to the highly advanced but infamous public failure, the APT (Advanced Passenger Train). The APT was an attempt to improve the speeds achieved by the Intercity 125 trains that still run today. This quest for improving train speeds has led to many of the innovations on the railway and has directly impacted on the passengers over the decades.

The speed of the APT was increased through the deployment of a controversial tilting mechanism, but after a series of problems and a loss of financial and political support, the APT project was soon abandoned. The patents for the tilting mechanism were sold to the railway division of FIAT in Italy, who were working on their own set of tilting trains. These patents were used to improve the designs and eventually the Italian Pendolino was born.

The Pendolino trains have received their fair share of criticism, much of it relating to the passenger experience. The seats are crammed in and there is little room to spread out. If you are lucky enough to get a seat that is near one of the few windows on board, the view is limited and there is nowhere comfortable to rest your arm. Many of these restrictions on passengers are derived from high-speed rail safety regulations, which particularly apply when trains cross one another in a tunnel. I wonder what the views of a Victorian traveller aboard a Pendolino might have been, if their only other experience of rail travel had been aboard one of Britain's first passenger trains?

The first recorded steam-powered device was the aeolipile, created in the first century AD, but it was in Britain during the eighteenth century that true advancements in steam power were made. Beginning

The Class 390 Pendolino is an electric high-speed train operated by Virgin Trains in the United Kingdom. It uses Fiat Ferroviaria's tilting train Pendolino technology and is built by Alstom.

OPPOSITE: The Advanced Passenger Train (APT) – this one pictured in 1972 – was a short-lived, early attempt to bring tilting train technology to Britain's railways.

with Thomas Savery's steam pump in 1689, improvements were steadily made in the technology and steam became inseparable from the industrial revolution. As steam power was harnessed to create rotary

> **"THE BENEFITS TO PEOPLE WHO TRAVELLED BY STEAM RAILWAY WERE THAT THIS METHOD OF TRAVEL WAS BOTH CHEAPER AND FASTER."**

motion and engines became lighter and more powerful, the idea of using a mobile steam engine that ran on rails became a reality.

As with any new technology, it took time to work out how to make passenger trains profitable. The Stockton and Darlington railway (1825) had one passenger carriage named 'Experiment' and although it was pulled by a steam engine during special ceremonies and the like, it was usually pulled by horse. Horse-drawn railways were not new, as the rails allowed the horse to pull a much heavier load. This could just as easily be people as goods. One such example is the short-lived Swansea to Mumbles horse-drawn passenger railway of 1807.

The Liverpool and Manchester Railway is considered by many to be the first true steam-hauled public railway service, featuring compartmentalized coaches and a proper timetable. The design of this railway's coaches influenced many others, and early passenger travel on the steam railways began. The benefits to people who travelled by steam railway were that this method of travel was both cheaper and faster. The drawback was that, at times, it could be very uncomfortable. The movement of the train itself could cause discomfort, and driving wind and rain often added to the misery of the passengers. Sometimes, during or after heavy downpours, water would slosh around the bottom of the carriages and soot, smoke and cinders from the engine would find their way into passengers' eyes or down their collars. However, this was the way of the future – and nothing was going to stop the railways.

BUILDING THE PERMANENT WAY

OPPOSITE: The InterCity 125 was the brand name of British Rail's High Speed Train (HST) fleet, which was built from 1975 to 1982 and was introduced in 1976.

Once it became apparent that the railways were the way forward, several companies formed and many railways were built. Not all came to fruition and not all were successful, but the one thing that all the companies had in common was that they needed someone to construct the track, known as the 'permanent way'. That someone was the 'navvy'.

The word 'navvy' is an abbreviation of 'navigator' and is synonymous with the construction of the British railways. By the end of the nineteenth century, one in every hundred people in the UK was a navvy. The work of navvies – labourers, essentially – is often equated with large historical building projects, such as the great pyramid at Giza. However, it is much harder to envision the scale of the railway navvies' work compared with that involved in a single-site construction project. Additionally, whereas an individual monument will often show evidence of an associated workers' village, the very nature of the permanent way meant that the transient camps that navvies established left little or no remaining trace on the landscape.

NAVVY CAMP

In order to better understand how navvies lived and worked, we travelled to Herefordshire, where Colin Richards had erected a navvy camp based on a nineteenth-century photograph. Stepping into the camp was like going back in time. We had certainly picked the day for it, as we had had a relatively mild winter but this was the first truly cold day. The night before temperatures had dropped as low as minus ten degrees, and during the day they never got above freezing. The surrounding countryside looked magical, with trees covered in a heavy frost, but it was so cold that even the smallest leaves hanging directly above the blacksmith's forge never thawed out.

My father used to say to me that '*any fool can be cold and wet*'. I have spent much of my life outdoors and have always heeded these words, but the one part of my body that I find the hardest to keep warm is my feet, especially when I am wearing hobnail boots. The metal studs seem to conduct the cold and no amount of socks ever seem to help.

We met Colin Richards next to the still. He was brewing up a carrot whisky and we had a glass as we talked about health and safety.

> **"THE WORK OF NAVVIES – LABOURERS, ESSENTIALLY – IS OFTEN EQUATED WITH LARGE HISTORICAL BUILDING PROJECTS, SUCH AS THE GREAT PYRAMID AT GIZA."**

The nineteenth-century navvies were relatively well paid when compared with farm labourers or factory workers, but they had to work very hard. They had a reputation for playing hard, too. It is

Presenter Ruth
Goodman looking out of
the train window on her
way to navvy camp.

OVERLEAF: Peter Ginn
and Alex Langlands
being welcomed by
Colin Richards at
the navvy camp.

a common misconception that the navvies were Irish. Although some navvies who worked on the railways came from Ireland, they represented only about ten per cent of the total number of men who worked on the permanent way.

Many of the navvies were local men, but the promise of good money also attracted seasonal workers, who often came from the farms that the railways disrupted. However, many workers were dedicated, full-time navvies who operated in groups known as gangs and followed the work around the countryside. These groups started out pretty small, but grew in size as the demand for railways increased.

Many established communities feared the arrival of the navvies, as they passed through villages and towns constructing the permanent way. They had no roots and were often viewed as having no religion. Their rough lifestyle, combined with a disposable income, meant that the local innkeepers were generally kept happy. However, the navvies had a reputation for fighting, and tensions between rival gangs competing for work were often settled in a bar room brawl.

Anyone who has ever visited Camden in north London has probably noticed the sheer amount of urban infrastructure there that is associated

with the railways. Camden was at one time quite a rural area, but the railways quickly changed that. The district lies in spitting distance of three of Britain's largest train stations: King's Cross, Euston and St Pancras. It also proudly boasts the Camden roundhouse, one of the oldest railway buildings to survive, and is criss-crossed by sidings, main lines and the underground.

To build all of this, navvies had to be in the area for a long time. Thus, in order to prevent trouble and to avoid injuries from fighting that might prevent a gang from working, multiple pubs were constructed to segregate the different nationalities. The four pubs in question were the Edinburgh castle, the Dublin castle, the Windsor castle (no longer a pub) and the Pembroke castle.

When navvies moved through towns or villages, they would generally stay in local lodgings. However, much of the urbanization we see associated with railway lines post-dates the lines being built. Indeed, much of the housing in Camden, especially around Primrose Hill, consists of cottages that were hastily erected in order to house railway workers.

Many of the navvies working on the permanent way would have found themselves effectively in the middle of nowhere, living in makeshift dwellings, and drinking homemade hooch, rather like Colin Richards' carrot whisky. As we sipped from our glasses and the burn in our throats fended off the chill in the air, Colin gave each of us a bowler hat.

In the mid-nineteenth century, life was cheap and health and safety was in its infancy. Industrial accidents were commonplace and a navvy's work was often dangerous, especially during the construction of tunnels or deep embankments. A navvy had to trust that the environment they were working in was as safe as possible. They also had to trust those around them – but ultimately they were responsible for their own safety.

The bowler hat was a popular choice of headgear amongst the Victorian working classes. The hat is believed to have been commissioned by Edward Coke (pronounced 'Cook'), who approached the London hatters Locke & Co. Coke wanted a hat for his gamekeepers at Holkham Hall that could withstand a blow from low hanging branches when they were on horseback and, if tales are to be believed, a thump over the head from a poacher's stick. The resulting stiff felt hat withstood Coke stamping on it twice and, satisfied with its strength, he replaced his gamekeepers' previous headgear of choice – the top hat.

The bowler hat does have other names, such as the Billycock or the Derby. One thing that is certain: it has become an iconic piece

Both the top hat and the bowler hat were originally designed with a practical, hard-wearing purpose in mind, as opposed to being mere fashion statements.

of headwear. It is very similar to a modern hardhat. It has a rim that gives the eyes protection from either debris falling from above or from catching yourself on a protruding nail when turning your head. It keeps the rain off and is relatively hard. If I were a navvy and had the choice, I would definitely have worn a bowler hat.

During the twentieth century, the bowler became synonymous with gentlemen working in the city. It is part of the guards' walkout uniform for officers, along with a pinstriped suit and a tightly furled umbrella. This has meant that the hat's original working class origins have faded. Indeed, while wearing my own bowler hat at navvy camp, I lost count of the number of people who, upon spying it, said to me 'you must be the foreman'. My reply was to inform them that if they ever travelled to South America they should try and visit one of the indigenous ethnic groups known collectively as the Quechuas. British railway workers introduced the hat to the continent in the 1920s, and to this day many of the Quechua women still wear bowler hats.

SAW MILL

One of our first jobs at the navvy camp was tarring sleepers. However, before we could do that we had to make the sleepers in the first place. The railways were a new technology. No one knew how a train powered by steam would behave as it moved along rails. In the early days (the 1830s) it was thought that the track had to be rigid. It is easy to see how that idea could gain credence, as powerful, heavy but inefficient engines moved slowly along the permanent way.

Early sleepers were made out of stone, and to ensure maximum rigidity these sleepers were often concreted into position. The rails that made the track were initially quite short and simply spanned the gap between the rigid sleepers. Stone was a cheaper material than wood, but as the railway technology rapidly progressed and rails were made longer, it soon became apparent that something had to give – both literally and economically! Although it was more expensive, the plain fact was that wood offered the extra degree of flexibility that was required by several tons of train and freight moving at speed.

So, in time, the stone sleepers were removed and wooden ones took their place. As an interesting aside, the spire at St Walburge's church in Preston is the third tallest spire in the UK after those of Salisbury and Norwich cathedrals (and the tallest spire of any parish church). It is constructed exclusively from the limestone sleepers that were removed from the Preston and Longridge Railway.

For many men in the nineteenth and early twentieth centuries, a bowler hat was part of standard everyday attire.

OVERLEAF: Presenters Peter Ginn and Alex Langlands making ready to fell a tree for the production of wooden railway sleepers.

In 2007, road excavations uncovered a number of intact stone sleepers that were used as long ago as 1825 for the Stockton and Darlington railway. These were the very first sleepers to be laid down and weighed only 75lb, so that they could be carried by one person. However, they soon proved to be too flimsy and were quickly replaced by larger ones. Most of the 64,000 original sleepers were destroyed, but some were used in a retaining wall and it was these that were uncovered during the works for the Darlington Eastern Transport Corridor.

The sheer number of main lines, branch lines and sidings mean that the total number of railway sleepers in use in Britain is absolutely colossal. In the 1930s, at arguably the height of Britain's railways in terms of infrastructure, the Great Western company owned an estimated 9,000 miles of track which equated to almost 20 million sleepers in use. However, sleepers, like rails, had to be replaced and during the same period the London, Midland and Scottish railway had an annual requirement of 1.25 million sleepers.

By the 1930s, sleeper production was big business, involving the mass importation of wood and extensive mechanical processing and treating. One hundred years earlier, it was a different story. Some early wooden sleepers were manufactured in the half round. This would mean harvesting young managed woodland, sawing the wood to length (which in the Victorian era was nine feet, becoming eight and a half feet in the twentieth century), and splitting the log in two. Splitting a log is a lot easier and quicker then sawing it, and if the tree has grown in relative shelter and the grain is straight, the split should result in a nice, flat face.

These half-round sleepers persisted for a while and crossed over with the uniform square-cut sleepers that are well known today. A type of wooden sleeper that was very short lived was the triangular sleeper, with the apex of the triangle driven down into the ballast stones. A triangle is the profile that one would achieve when splitting a tree with a much larger circumference into sleeper-sized chunks. The problem with split wood is that each face is unique and will be governed by the grain. Mass production requires order and uniformity. The nine-foot wooden sleeper with a square-cut end of ten by five inches was quickly adopted as standard.

The permanent way had to be as level as possible, as trains struggle with inclines and steep gradients are out of the question. The steepest sustained gradient on Britain's railways, that does not employ a third rail for traction like a fell system, is Lickey Incline. At two miles long, it has a gradient of 1 in 37.7 or 2.65 per cent. Steam trains ascending this incline

would often need bankers, which are other steam engines, to help them push their load uphill.

The creation of the permanent way involved building bridges, boring tunnels, digging cuttings and compiling embankments. As the navvies constructed the permanent way across a landscape that had not been significantly altered since the time of James I, they encountered many obstacles that either had to be avoided or demolished.

Often the navvies would have to remove trees that could be used as sleepers. Hardwoods such as oak were the most sought after for this purpose. At navvy camp, we felled an oak tree in order to cut it into sleepers. When felling a tree you must first look at the landscape and decide which way you want the tree to fall. You need to consider other trees and whether the branches will catch them as the felled tree falls down. The wind will always be a factor, and when we felled our oak, the wind speed was high. However, due to the size of the tree, we could fell it directly into the wind.

Once you have decided on the direction in which you want the tree to fall, you need to cut a notch known as a 'gob'. I have always been taught, when felling with a two-man saw, to cut the horizontal bottom cut first. This is a very important cut and worth taking the time to get right, as this will determine the way in which the tree falls. It is essential to keep the saw level and have the perpendicular line formed by the cut to be in the direction you wish the tree to fall. Then, using a felling axe, the gob can be cut out by chopping down onto the cut you have made in the tree.

Once the gob has been created, a cut from the other side of the tree is made in order to fell it. It is important to establish lines of safety. Anywhere in front of the tree is a no-go area and directly behind the tree is also dangerous – both because a tree can fall the wrong way, but also because a tree when falling can kick backwards. The accepted safe paths are on each side of a tree at 120 degrees to the direction of the intended fall. The safest place to stand is behind the nearest big tree.

Cutting a tree down to make way for a railway is only half the story. The real problem is the stump. Victorian stumps were usually a lot higher than modern tree stumps, because of how a two-man saw was used. However, even if the stump was cut down to ground level, laying track over the top of it would only result in serious problems later on, when the stump rotted out or the tree tried to grow back (often from the roots).

In market gardening, tree stumps were often removed mechanically or by the use of an explosive such as stumping powder or dynamite. The navvies working on the permanent way were more likely to dig down into the ground around the stump, set a fire and smother the whole thing in leaf litter and earth. The result would be a clamp that would burn the remaining stump into charcoal. This could then be used as fuel for blacksmithing or simply for domestic fires. Although many trees were cut down to meet the demands of the railways, no part of the tree was ever wasted.

Once our tree was on the ground, we could get round to processing it. The first job is to remove the branches and is known as 'snedding'. The trunk can then be cut into sections, with the objective of obtaining

"IN MARKET GARDENING, TREE STUMPS WERE OFTEN REMOVED MECHANICALLY OR BY THE USE OF AN EXPLOSIVE SUCH AS STUMPING POWDER."

as many nine-foot sleepers as possible firmly in mind. To cut the trunk sections into sleepers, we used Britain's only working water-powered saw mill, on the Gunton estate in Norfolk, just outside Cromer.

Peter and Alex stand over the felled tree. A two-man saw necessarily leaves quite a high stump. This then needs to be removed.

The beautiful rural setting of Gunton saw mill near Cromer, Norfolk, which is still in operation to this day.

Built in 1824, just before Britain's railway bonanza, by the third Lord Suffield, the saw mill is a remarkable building housing a remarkable piece of kit. It was originally intended to be used as a processing plant for all of the estate's timber, and just outside the doors of the building are the remnants of hastily poured concrete that represented the additional two circular saw pits made by the allies during the Second World War.

However, by the mid-1970s the building had completely fallen into disrepair. The thatch had started to rot, there had been a fire, and the two-and-a-half ton cast-iron flywheel had fallen from its mountings. The Norfolk county council, the local windmill trust and industrial archaeology society collectively drew up plans. With the help of the last remaining tenanted Harbord family member, Doris – and after her passing, the estate's new owner Mr Kit Martin – the water-powered saw mill was saved.

When Alex and I first entered the building, he noted the recently thatched roof. Between the thatch and the rafters was a layer of woven reeds – known as 'fleeking' – that Alex commented upon. I told him that I had once lived in a thatched building and it too had been f-ing leaking…!

One of the notable aspects of the Gunton saw mill was just how dry the building was inside considering that there were two huge water wheels at the back. The sides of the building are wooden slatted panels that can be removed to increase light and more importantly to create an opening through which the tree trunk to be processed can be passed. I found the hardest aspect of the whole process to be moving the trunk from the yard outside to the saw bench. We used block and tackle, which through a series of pulleys gives the rope being pulled a mechanical advantage. We hauled the log in and got it set on the bench. After that, the saw mill did all the work.

The water power for the saw mill comes from a man-made lake that covers close to forty acres. We lifted the sluice gate and filled the headrace that channels the water onto the wheels inside. There are two wheels, one to drive our saw and one to power a grain crusher. They idly turn just on the water that leaks through the gaps. The benefit of this is that it stops the paddles of the wheel drying out and splitting and prevents an imbalance in the wheel between a wet and a dry side. A sluice gate for each wheel that regulates the flow of water is operated from inside. These effectively act as throttles for the wheels, but even when we fully opened the gates and had the wheels turning at full pelt, there was very little noise.

An ancient rural water wheel and mill with a substantial water source in the foreground.

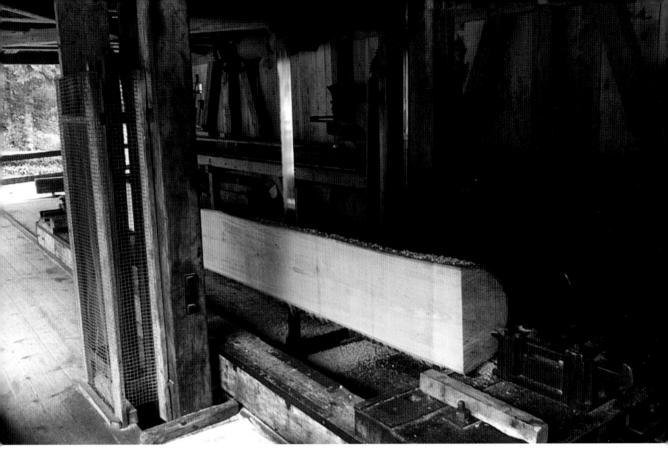

A powered frame saw of the type that would have been used for cutting wooden railway sleepers in the nineteenth century.

The wheels are 'breast-shot', which means that the water hits the paddles of the wheel at about the height of the axle and runs underneath the wheel. Early water wheels tended to be 'undershot' wheels, which sat on a stream or a river and utilized the kinetic energy. The most powerful water wheels are 'overshot' wheels, which use both the kinetic and gravitational potential energy of water flowing into them. Breast-shot wheels are found in places like Gunton, where the landscape does not naturally provide a height advantage. However, the funnelling of a huge millpond into a narrow millrace changes the pressure created by the weight of the water into velocity.

The saw itself was exactly the same as a pit saw, except instead of being worked by two people – one standing at the top and the other at the bottom – this saw was fitted to a large frame that moved up and down. We only had one saw in place, but when cutting planks it was possible to fix multiple saws at set distances. The key was to make sure that they were all exactly aligned.

As the saw moved up and down, the gearing designed by a clock maker could be engaged. Similar to an escapement mechanism in a pendulum clock, this periodically turns an axle attached to two pinion gears, which moved two racks attached to the underside of the frame upon which the log to be cut was chained. This moved the log through the saw a fraction of an inch at a time. As the log passed through the saw, the chains and the cross-struts of the frame were removed and re-attached so that the saw only cut the log. This was relatively straightforward, but nevertheless we set the saw at the lowest speed. I was told it was frightening when the saw was going at full pelt.

Just as with a pit saw, as the log went through we tapped thin wedges into the cut to open it up and stop the wood biting the saw. However, unlike a pit saw, we did not need to chalk a line for the cut. Instead, plumb bobs were used to eye up the cut of the saw, but once the log was strapped in their was no deviation to the cutting line. When a log is first put on the frame to be cut, it is strapped to a plank to give it some stability. Once a face has been cut, the log can be turned onto it and it becomes steady.

These water-powered frame saws were reasonably common throughout Europe and there were a number in Norfolk. However, pit saw workers did not welcome them, because they rendered many men redundant. They were also short lived, because circular saws took over and steam power followed by diesel and electricity became the power sources of choice. The mill at Gunton survived because of its position on an estate isolating it from the outside world and because it was never taken over commercially.

The last job we had to do was to jump down into the saw pit and empty out the saw dust. It was in no way strenuous and because it was all oak shavings the saw dust could be used for smoking meats. However, it was a dirty job, with dust getting everywhere. We wore paper hats that are made simply from sheets of broadsheet newspaper. These hats are easy to make, disposable and protect your hair from the dust that can be easily brushed off or rinsed off from other parts of your body.

These paper hats would have been a common sight in Victorian Britain and are very similar to the hats worn today by people involved in the food processing industry. Sir John Tenniel, the political cartoonist who illustrated Lewis Carroll's *Alice's Adventures in Wonderland* and *Through the Looking Glass*, depicts the carpenter wearing a paper hat in

A self-portrait of Sir John Tenniel, the celebrated Victorian artist and author of 'The Walrus and the Carpenter'.

The Walrus and the Carpenter – the latter in his paper hat. John Tenniel's acutely observed social and political commentaries were highly regarded during his lifetime.

OVERLEAF: Nineteenth-century railway workers repairing sleepers. Building and maintaining the early railways of Britain involved a lot of hard, physical labour.

his illustration of the poem 'The Walrus and the Carpenter'. Tenniel's collective works are considered important to the study of that period's social history. Mr Chip the carpenter in *Happy Families* also wears a paper hat, but it is thought – although he is not credited – that the *Happy Families* drawings were done by Tenniel.

As we took our oak sleepers back to the navvy camp, I wondered just how many sleepers the Gunton saw mill had produced for the railways. One of the problems with wooden sleepers is that they rot. The oak sleepers we had made were highly sought after, because hardwoods such as oak lasted a long time as did pitch pine, but many of the imported sleepers were made of softwoods that did not last long. The railways adopted a variety of different approaches to this problem.

One solution was 'Kyanizing' – a process initially patented in 1832 by its inventor and namesake, John Howard Kyan. Kyan, who at one point worked in a vinegar factory, developed a way of pickling wood in mercury chloride. The process gained a lot of public attention at the same time as the railways were battling their wood preservation issues.

Other companies would let sleepers just rot out and replace them when they needed to, but many covered them with substances such as coal tar or, like us today, bitumen. Bitumen is a hydrocarbon that sits between coal and oil. Its semi-solid state means that if you were to leave a block of bitumen – which breaks like glass when hit with a hammer – on the floor of your garage, it would eventually turn into a puddle shape. The largest known natural deposit of bitumen is in Canada in Alberta, which covers an area of 55,000 square miles – greater than the entire area of England.

However, the nineteenth-century British navvies who covered railway sleepers in natural bitumen may well have got their supplies from the tar tunnel in Ironbridge in Shropshire, before it dried up in 1847. This large bitumen deposit was first discovered in 1787, when a canal tunnel was being constructed near Coalport in the Ironbridge gorge. The focus of the project shifted from tunnel construction to bitumen mining and initially over 4,000 gallons of the material were collected each week. This soon tailed off, however, and by the 1820s only ten barrels of bitumen a year were being produced.

In order for us to apply the bitumen to the sleepers, we first had to break it up with a hammer. We then put it in a copper over a fire and heated it until it became liquid. The wood we were using was broken up pieces of floorboard, joists and lath. Much of the wood was covered in paint. This was similar to the wood the navvies used, because much of it came from houses that were demolished to make way for the railways.

The permanent way was constructed from point A to point B. Prior to any track being laid or any spades being put in the ground, teams of surveyors were sent out into the landscape to determine the best routes. Some wealthy landowners welcomed the railways, because they had either already invested in them or they saw their potential. However, many landowners were opposed to them. One such landowner was the Earl of Harborough, who objected to a railway proposed by George Stephenson passing through his estate, Stapleford Park.

The Earl had a financial interest in a nearby canal and believed the competition from the railway would have a negative effect. He refused to sell his land, the Midland Railway men refused to take 'no' for an answer, and skirmishes broke out involving almost 300 people. The dispute became known as the 'Battle of Saxby'. The railway was eventually built, but it had to travel around Stapleford Park in a huge bend known as 'Lord Harborough's Curve' (*see* box overleaf).

Railways had to respect rights of way and bridges, underpasses and crossings all had to be considered when dissecting an existing route. The railways also had to consider the welfare of animals as they passed

LORD HARBOROUGH'S CURVE

For over twenty years, the words 'Lord Harborough's Curve' were uttered in irritation by passengers travelling at a snail's pace through part of the East Midlands. It was a phrase that continued in wider use to conjure up the intransigence of vested interests and carried much the same condemnatory connotation as the modern acronym, NIMBY ('not in my back yard'). Lord Harborough was one of many aristocrats and wealthy landowners who tried to divert the new railway lines away from his estate. However, his personal conflict with the railway promoters caused more fuss than most.

Lord Harborough owned a very nice, landscaped park around his main residence, located between Leicester and Peterborough. The trees planted by his ancestors had matured and formed pleasing avenues and copses. Thirty years previously, Harborough had invested heavily in a canal which passed through this park quietly and unobtrusively, providing for all his estate transport needs and generating a healthy income. The prospect of a railway with all the attendant dirt and noise (and early railways *were* exceedingly noisy in comparison to modern ones, due to the short sections of jointed track and loose coupling of wagons) right through the middle of his park, close to the house and in competition with his interest in his commercial canal was not a welcome one.

Standing in Stapleford Hall (now a luxury hotel) and looking out across the park, you can see his point. You probably would not fancy the tranquillity of the area being shattered by an early railway, either. If you are one of those people who is going to be affected by the proposed HS2 railway line, you will have a fairly clear idea of what motivated Lord Harborough to dig in his heels.

In order to build a line across the countryside, a railway company had to obtain an act of parliament that allowed them to compulsorily purchase the land. For pretty much the first time in history, an aristocratic landowner did not have final say over his land. However, in order to get an act through parliament, the railway promoters had to present evidence of a feasible route, and for this they needed a survey of the land. Lord Harborough refused the surveyors access, and with just twenty-four days to get the work done, the pressure was on.

Word went out to local gamekeepers and estate workers that surveyors were to be kept off the land. Bands of thugs and even a prizefighter were hired from the local pubs to assist in the defence of the estate. Meanwhile, the surveyors hired their own 'guards' as they attempted to gain access, legally or otherwise. Things came to a head after several smaller confrontations upon the towpath of the canal in what the local press called 'The Battle of Saxby'. Pushing became shoving, punches were thrown, equipment was broken and men fell into Lord Harborough's canal.

Nevertheless, these bouts of rough stuff could not stop the surveyors. They sneaked into the estate over the next few days and got just enough measurements in order to make their case. Lord Harborough settled for a very considerable compensation settlement (and maybe that is what he was really after all along) and a binding agreement to hide the railway in a tunnel as it passed across his estate.

However, this was not quite the end of the story. The tunnel was constructed in what was geologically completely unsuitable land and collapsed during construction, taking many of Lord Harborough's precious trees with it. Instead, the railway was eventually built in a ridiculously tight curve, following the boundary wall of Stapleford Park, which forced trains to slow down to a crawl for this section of their journey. Lord Stapleford's view along with his peace and quiet were preserved at the expense of everyone else's convenience. That remained the case until his death, when his heir proved only too

willing to sell the railway a slice of the park at a big, fat profit, so that they could smooth off the corner with a new section of straighter track.

All in all, land purchases and compensation payments have been estimated to have cost the various railway companies something in the region of four times the contemporary value of the land. The more direct the route they insisted upon, the greater the need for surveying speed – and the more the railways were willing to simply buy their way out of trouble with landowners.

The same could not be said for tenants – particularly poor urban tenants who frequently found themselves out on the street with little warning and no compensation as the railways punched their way through working class housing and into the centre of Britain's towns and cities. With no alternative housing on offer, many poorer people

A contemporary view of Stapleford Park, which is now a luxury country hotel. In the mid-nineteenth century, this Leicestershire estate was notorious as an early example of 'nimbyism', due to its owner's intransigence in the face of the rampaging railways.

who were affected had to crowd ever more tightly into already insanitary overcrowded slums. Nor was there any compensation for those who now found their doors, yards and windows a matter of feet from passing trains. Working class districts were carved up by viaducts, embankments and cuttings, to be peered into by passing passengers. Passengers who included men like Friedrich Engels and Karl Marx, who were formulating new ideas about society, economics and history based upon what they saw of British industrial urban life. The railways both created many of our nation's worst slums and displayed them to middle class view, prompting social reformers of many political hues to action.

The far-reaching social and economic effects of the emerging railway network were not lost on the leading social commentators of the day, such as Friedrich Engels.

through farmland. Much of the track needed to be enclosed with stock-proof fencing. (Interestingly, some of the fencing in the West Country was made out of Brunel's old wide gauge rails, once the gauge had been standardized to a smaller width). George Stephenson did remark that an accident would '*be the worse for the cow*', but a train hitting an animal would also have a detrimental effect on the engine.

Often farmers had to be paid compensation for the loss and alteration of their land. At the farm at Acton Scott where we lived for a year filming *Victorian Farm*, there was a building called Cray Barn adjacent to

Peter Ginn and Alex Langlands prepare to tar their wooden railway sleepers.

OVERLEAF: Peter and Alex spreading bitumen on the sleepers, with Colin Richards looking on.

the now disused branch line. The villagers still proudly remember the night that the Royal train parked up on that very stretch of line. The line cuts the farmer's grazing effectively in two, and Cray Barn was built by the railway as a location where he could over-winter his cattle, so that he did not have to bring the herd to the other side of the tracks and back to the main farm.

Many railways often travelled through slums on the edges of cities. The railways cutting through these slums often gave many people their first glimpse of working class living conditions that had largely been created by the industrial revolution. It was a period of huge social change and with it social reform and commentary, such as the 1845 publication *The Condition of the Working Class in England*, by the German social scientist Friedrich Engels.

The slum dwellings in cities that were in the way of proposed railways were often easier to demolish than the newly emerging suburbs. However, they were also harder to cut through than a country estate, due to the presence of multiple property owners. I lived in a house in London that was in a Georgian terrace. The part of the terrace I was in had been demolished in order for a cut and cover tunnel to be built. The houses had then been rebuilt to a Victorian floor plan and a lesser quality, but with a Georgian exterior. All of these houses and slums would have yielded a large quantity of pre-cut wood that was perfect for lighting the many fires needed to build the railways.

The fumes were acrid and the cold was not our friend. I would take out a ladle full of bitumen, having first heated the metal ladle. I then poured it on each side of the sleeper in turn as Alex followed me with the brush to smooth it off. However, the sleepers were so cold that our workable window of fluid bitumen was not much more than one or two seconds.

When heated, bitumen is very flammable. We did manage to set fire to the brush, but this only made matters worse. However, we were pleased with the final result. It took us a few sleepers to get our eye in and perfect our technique, but soon we had a system that worked. As a child, I remember seeing sleepers covered with bitumen that were no longer on the

> "THE FUMES WERE ACRID AND THE COLD WAS NOT OUR FRIEND. I WOULD TAKE OUT A LADLE FULL OF BITUMEN, HAVING FIRST HEATED THE METAL LADLE."

railways. One of the benefits of bitumen is that it is semi-liquid, so any cracks that form when it is cold will heal when the sun comes out. This also allows the timber to breathe and the moisture to escape as it seasons in situ.

The bitumen definitely kept the rain off, as any moisture that landed on the sleepers balled up into droplets. Most railway companies treated their sleepers themselves and, due to the vast numbers needed, the process became mechanized. The preferred treatment ended up being creosote. There are two types of creosote; one derived from wood tar that was often used in the preservation of foods and one derived from coal tar, used for the preservation of materials such as wood. They are chemically different. The creosote was forced into the sleepers under pressure and when the treatment was finished each sleeper would contain over ten litres of the stuff.

RENOWNED NAVVIES

We stepped into the living accommodation that Colin had built for a cup of tea. It was often the youngest navvy's job to make the tea. Each navvy would have their own tea and sugar in a tin and the nipper would collect some from each person and make the brew. This ritual became known as 'drumming up', as the 'tea pot' was any metal vessel and was referred to as a drum. This expression was also used in the Glasgow shipyards.

There are plenty of accounts of navvies digging holes in the ground to sleep in or just lying down and sleeping rough wherever they could. The thought of this made Colin's bunkhouse seem positively homely. Navvies lived on top of each other and many had their families with them. The camp they set up by the side of the railway lines they were building could often become insanitary, and outbreaks of dysentery or worse were common. In the short time we were sitting having tea, we could see condensation form on the tin roof and begin to run down over the bed.

The navvies, who also built the canals and worked on the docks, were almost a sub-working class. Despite paying them a good wage, many of the companies that employed the men took advantage. Rather than paying the navvies in money, they would pay them in goods or coupons to spend in the truck shop, which sold items at inflated prices. By the nineteenth century this practice had largely ceased, although navvies were still encouraged to spend their cash in the truck shops. Children born to navvies began work at a young age. One of the first jobs was ferrying tools back and forth and taking them to the blacksmith's shop for sharpening. As the boys got older they became 'fat-boys', so named for the grease they smeared on the axles of carts and wagons.

Navvies from different parts of the country had different nicknames. Navvies from Wales were called 'mountain-pecker', those from Lancashire were called 'Lanks', but my favourite is the name given to navvies from Wiltshire. This was 'moonrakers', after the folk tale of how a group of Wiltshire men hid French brandy from customs officers in a village pond. When they tried to retrieve it at night and were caught by the custom officials, they explained their actions by saying they were trying to rake in the giant cheese that was in the pond. The officials, seeing the cheese in question was a reflection of the moon, deemed them yokels and let them be.

We could see the moon from where we were sitting, and Colin's bed did look inviting – but we still had work to do. In order to attach the iron chairs, in which the rails sit, to the sleepers, we had to make coach bolts. The coach bolts that are used today are very similar to the early coach bolts used in the railways, except that the first coach bolts were all mass-produced by hand by teams of blacksmiths. They are relatively simple devices. A piece of iron is upset at one end. The resulting bulge is then squared off to form a nut. The shaft of the bolt is also squared off in the middle and then heated and twisted to form the screw. Finally, the end of the piece is drawn out to a point. The final result is a piece of iron, that although unique looks identical to every other one that has been made. This can then be hammered and twisted into the wooden sleeper below.

As the coach bolt fizzed in the 'bosh' of the sleeper, we thought about all those traditional crafts that had come together to build the railways. The railways unified the country, allowed for greater mobility and standardized time. Villages that had once been remote now found themselves linked to the outside world via a train to London – and then, if you had the money, a train on to Dover with a ticket for a paddle steamer. Village identity in Britain was truly unique. The varying regional styles of the simple tool the bill hook attest to that localized identity. Navvies travelling as they worked would have been acutely aware of the regional variations. They were also aware of the changes in soil and

> **"THE COACH BOLTS THAT ARE USED TODAY ARE VERY SIMILAR TO THE EARLY COACH BOLTS USED IN THE RAILWAYS AND MADE BY BLACKSMITHS."**

Railway navvies working a brickmaking machine during the construction of the Midland Railway's St Pancras Station in London, August 1867.

geological stratigraphy. There are even arguments proposed that the navvies were among the first to identify stratigraphy in an archaeological sense, as many would have been employed on antiquarian excavations.

However, the railways would go some way in eroding the different regional identities of Britain. It was a period of huge change in the country. Even the navvies, who were perceived as godless and pursued by missions, were affected. *The Times* newspaper led the way in reaching mass circulation, using a steam-driven rotary press and adopting steam trains as a way of boosting readership. 'The Thunderer', as it was affectionately known, also introduced the practice of dispatching war correspondents. The reports by W. H. Russell on the Crimea War caused shock and outrage to the readers back home. The Crimea engraved images of the charge of the light brigade, Florence Nightingale, and balaclavas on the national consciousness. It was one of the first conflicts to deploy naval shells, telegraph wires and railways.

To build the railway between Balaklava and Sebastopol Peto, the building contractors Brassey and Betts recruited huge gangs of navvies and took them to the Crimea. Reports appeared back home of how the navvies worked day and night through rain, hail and snow, laying the

Navvies employed by Thomas Brassey, working on the construction of the railway between Balaklava and Sebastopol Peto during the Crimean War, 1853–1856.

track at a fantastic rate. *The Illustrated London News* suggested one solution to the conflict was to send in the navvies in hand-to-hand combat. The public came to admire the navvies and many pictures of the period showed that the men departing were leaving behind families.

Thomas Brassey was one of the best contractors the navvies could work for. Brassey built some 6,500 miles of railway in total, which equates to one in twenty miles of track in the whole world. During his busiest periods, Brassey had over 100,000 men in his employ and he made strenuous efforts to look after them properly. He subsidized hospitals, tried to stagger work to cover periods of inactivity and unemployment, and banned the beer sellers and tommy (food) shops. The statistic that a navvy could move twenty tonnes of earth in a day is an often-quoted figure. It is upon the efforts of Brassey's exceptional workforce that this figure is based.

STONE CRUSHING

As the navvies moved across the British landscape, they often encountered large rocks blocking their path. Moving such boulders requires a lot of effort and small stones were also needed as ballast. To deal with the problem, navvies employed the ancient technique of fire setting.

A technique that has been used in mining since prehistoric times, fire setting involves a fire being built in and around the rock that gradually heats the stone. While this happens, the first cracks begin to appear. When the rock is hot enough, the fire can be moved off and the rock can be rapidly doused in cold water. The resulting thermal shock causes the rock to fracture further. When we tried this technique, the results were astounding. The rock cracked into many pieces and when we struck it with the hammer it broke easily. Our earlier attempts to strike the rock with the hammer when it was cold did not even make a dent.

Ballast was essential for the railways. It is the crushed stone that the sleepers are bedded into. Ballast not only anchors the sleepers and the track in place – it helps spread the load on the rails and provides drainage to stop the sleepers rotting and the permanent way becoming waterlogged. This is very important, because insufficient ballast will result in problems with the ground and a possible destabilizing of the track.

As much as fire-cracked stones and clinker and slag from furnaces could be used as ballast, the demand by the railways for the material was so great that they had to turn to quarries. Initially, local stone was employed as ballast on the railways, but it was soon demonstrated that soft stones such as limestone began to round off and quickly wear away where they lay. One of the stones of choice was basalt, which is basically a Latin term meaning 'very hard rock'. When basalt is crushed, the angular stones lock together when put in place.

We travelled to Blodwell stone quarry in north Wales, on the county border with

An old Barrow steel rail, laying across a standard sleeper and bedded into mixed ballast.

Shropshire, where basalt stone for ballast was extracted up until the 1990s. Basalt is an igneous rock and is one of the most common rock types in the world. It was taken out of this quarry using rock drills driven by compressed air and explosives. A matrix of holes are drilled and explosives inserted, and then a face is blasted. The quarry was an impressive landscape, with a huge lake at its heart, surrounded by the manmade rock shelves known as 'chairs'.

Rock drills made by the Holman brothers running off compressors became a staple of mining and large-scale quarrying in the nineteenth century. Compressed air generated by steam power also powered the winch we used to move the carts containing our large lumps of basalt up to the rock crusher. The winch had previously been used on a steam ship. To get the stone into the rock crusher, we used our shovels.

The rock crusher was powered by a static steam engine via a canvas belt. We had problems with the steam engine creeping forward and the tension in the belt changing, but it was nothing that was not easily fixed. The crusher itself was a fairly basic, relentless machine. It had funnel-shaped jaws that oscillated, moving the rock upwards as gravity fed it down. The jaws could be set to produce the desired size of ballast and the resulting crushed rocks fell into another wagon, ready to be wheeled off on the rails to the desired location on the permanent way.

After crushing our rock, I went to check on the meal we had made. If you are cooking over an open fire, a good way to prepare food, especially fish, is to wrap it in dock leaves or moss and then encase it in clay. This package can then be left in a fire to cook while you go off to do other things. The Victorian diet contained more calories than the recommended modern

Presenters Peter Ginn and Alex Langlands standing in front of the steam-driven rock crusher *Oberon*.

diet, but the Victorians were more physically active than we are today. Navvies would have needed even more calories to give them the energy required to carry out their strenuous work. Sometimes, when they were in isolated areas of Britain, navvies would have cooked whatever came to hand.

KEIGHLEY AND WORTH VALLEY RAILWAY

We had cut our sleepers, we had crushed our ballast and we had created our coach bolts. All that was left was to see how they were combined to create the permanent way. We travelled to the Keighley and Worth Valley Railway in West Yorkshire, where the preservation society were replacing some of the rails on their line.

The Keighley and Worth Valley Railway opened in 1867, with much of its funding coming from local mill owners who needed a railway to serve the textile industry in the area. It soon became part of the Midland Railway. Then, later on in 1923, when the grouping occurred, it became part of the London, Midland and Scottish Railway.

In 1948 when the railways were nationalized, the Keighley and Worth Valley Railway was run by British Rail. Then in 1962, when it was deemed unprofitable, it was finally closed. This was met by a lot of local opposition and a preservation group quickly formed. The group acquired the railway and it reopened in 1968, but even in the short time that the railway had been out of commission, it had decayed badly. Vandals had caused much damage and harsh weather had taken its toll on the exposed rolling stock and engines. The society got the railway up and running again and it is now quite unique in Britain. Most preserved railways are only part of a line that once existed, but the KAWVR offers the whole branch line as it was.

However, we were not in West Yorkshire to play with trains – we were there to help lay track. We met Keith and Margaret, who were getting the crane ready to be taken out to be used to move the rails. The crane was a thing of beauty. It was built in 1942 and acquired from British rail in 1982. It was still fully operational, so needed very little

> **"THE KEIGHLEY AND WORTH VALLEY RAILWAY OPENED IN 1867, WITH MUCH OF ITS FUNDING COMING FROM LOCAL MILL OWNERS."**

THE FUTURE THAT MIGHT HAVE BEEN

In taking part in this project – examining how steam railways changed Britain – I have become acutely aware that a number of paths could have been taken and the best ideas did not always succeed.

The railways were created and improved over such a short period of time that early locomotives or carriages soon gave way to newer versions. Many of the early examples of rolling stock were not kept in service – and why would they be? In archaeology, a challenge that often presents itself is how to deal with a lack of material culture. Contrarily, we have a very defined version of railway history, but it could have been so very different....

Atmospheric railways

Nature abhors a vacuum – and that is why vacuum brakes were so successful. It is also the reason why from 1836 onwards pneumatic tube systems were used in many offices and banks to send messages and items from one location to another. The use of differential air pressure as a form of propulsion on a greater scale has long been seen as a possibility, but ultimately has never become an effective reality. The idea first gained merit early on, when steam engines were too heavy to effectively travel by rail. To have a static engine generate a vacuum that could pull a train seemed a fitting idea.

Perhaps the most famous attempted application was that of the celebrated Victorian engineer Isambard Kingdom Brunel, who engineered the Great Western Railway. His railway, which had reached as far as Exeter, was broad gauge – evidence of which can still be seen today at stations such as Taunton, where there is a visible space between the standard gauge tracks. Continuing westwards, the landscape became quite challenging. Steam locomotives run very well on level track but struggle with elevations. The track that runs down through the West Country stretching down to Cornwall is slightly bumpy at best. However, atmospheric railways can cope with slopes a lot better, and Brunel's ultimately aborted attempt at one was a fine early example of this technology.

George Medhurst was arguably the first to suggest the possibility of a commercial atmospheric railway, and many tried to make this a reality. However, the first commercially operated atmospheric railway was that found on the line to Dalkey, which was part of the Dublin and Kingston Railway. This was witnessed by many rail pioneers of the time and led Isambard kingdom Brunel to operate the South Devon railway as an atmospheric railway for a year. Despite the achievement of respectable speeds on the rails, sadly the innovation was ultimately not to be. It was a flawed system. Today, the putative concept of a vacuum system combined with magnetic levitation is still on the drawing board, with proponents advocating a new form of propulsion for entering space and the idea being part of the proposed hyperloop train.

Tracked hovercraft

At the very end of the age of steam, in the 1960s, a new transportation idea gained momentum. This was a hovercraft that ran on rails. Using hovercraft technology and an invention known as a 'linear induction motor', tracked hovercraft were set to become Britain's answer to high speed travel.

For a short while, the proposed concept looked like a winner – but it lost investment and found itself positioned between the idea of Maglev trains (those employing magnetic levitation) and the development of the Advanced Passenger Train (see page 74). The remains of the project can be glimpsed by passengers on board the east coast line as they pass by Peterborough. What is left of the RTV (research test vehicle) 31 is exhibited near to the entrance of 'Railworld'. RTV 31 clocked 104mph in 20mph headwinds on a one-mile section of track. At one time, it could have been the future....

work to be done. The BR colours of blue and yellow had been changed back to the deep green of the London and North Eastern Railway, and the iron floor of the cab had been replaced, because the alkaline leeching out of the ash from the boiler had worn the metal paper-thin.

A war department 2-10-0 steam locomotive making its way along the Keighley and Worth Valley railway.

The first thing we were given was a rag. Keith told us this was the most important thing and to always keep it to hand. Operating any steam machine is a dirty job and having a rag to wipe your hands upon is essential. The dirty rags covered in coal dust, oil and grease are then used to light the fire the next time the machine is used.

The crane was shunted out of the Victorian shed so that the fire could be lit. The shed still has all its original Victorian timbers supporting a stone-tiled roof and the fire risk is too great to light the fire indoors. It takes several hours to light a boiler and get it up to temperature. Often boilers of engines were never allowed to cool fully, so that the process was faster and the stress placed on the surrounding fabric was reduced.

We made sure that the water was topped up and the ash was raked out. We put a bed of coal on the grate and wood on top and then we placed a shovel of coal, wood and burning oil rags into the centre of the firebox. As the fire drew and the coal began to take light and the

Social historian Ruth Goodman in the guard's van of a train on the Keighley and Worth Valley Railway.

water temperature increased, we undertook the job of checking, oiling and greasing the crane. In the case of machinery such as this crane, you can never have too much lubricant. If there was any doubt that a grease point had been missed, we just added a bit more. Some of the moving parts had little reservoirs that fed thick oil into the works via wicks that worked using capillary action. Capillary action is a liquid's ability to move up or along a narrow space and was first observed by Leonardo da Vinci in the sixteenth century.

Once the moving parts were oiled, the boiler was up to pressure and we were ready to move the crane. Not a simple task, as it turned out. We were in a siding and had to negotiate our way onto the branch line. The steam in the crane powers the derrick or arm of the crane up and down, turns the crane round and raises and lowers the winch. It can also power the crane itself, so that the crane can move up and down the rails. However, unlike a steam engine, the boiler cannot issue steam while making steam. This means that when travelling to and from a site where the crane is needed, it has to be moved by a locomotive.

We knew the locomotive that was going to pull us, we knew where the guard's van was and we knew which flat bed we needed to take with us. More importantly, we knew the order the vehicles had to be in. Thus ensued a game of organize-that-train, as rolling stock that was not required was moved out of the way and vehicles that were required were moved to a suitable location.

Shunting would have happened on sidings in goods yards such as this on an almost continuous basis while the railways were in operation. Shunting can be very dangerous work and is quite physical. Indeed, to save fuel, many shunting yards were equipped with a windlass, so that wagons could be manually moved from siding to siding.

The section of track we were laying was to be located at the far end of the branch line. The term 'permanent way' (often abbreviated to 'p-way') was adopted in the early days of the railway to distinguish it from the temporary rails that many companies and navvies would lay to assist in the building of the tracks that would remain once work was finished. The network that was left comprised of sidings, branch lines and main lines. These were usually labelled 'up' and 'down' lines. The up line travels towards a major destination such as London or Edinburgh and the down line travels in the opposite direction. This is terminology that originated in mining, with carts going up to the mine or down to the port.

After an enjoyable journey along the line, we arrived at the section of track that needed replacing. A square red flag on two poles denoted the danger on the line where the rails had been removed. Once the gang had greeted us and our presence was known, the crane was moved along the other line into position. We were uncoupled from the rest of the train and we took off the locks that stopped the crane rotating unintentionally.

We made sure that the water in the boiler was topped up and the fire stoked and then we began work. The crane is now fitted with a modern electronic gauge to indicate safe working loads in relation to the angle and the rotation of the crane. The gauge does exactly the same job as the brass disc engraved with the same information. A needle that is attached to worm screws points to the relevant section as the crane moves, in order to alert the operator as to the precise load capacities that can be moved.

The rails that we had been tasked to put in place did not look very heavy from where I was sitting in the cab. However, they actually weighed around two and a half tons each. The thickness of the steel rails and the spacing of the sleepers dictate the speeds and weights of the trains that can use the railways. As trains travel over the rails, they begin to wear

Railway workers laying track in Kent. Rails can wear quickly – depending on the amount of use they undergo – and need constant maintenance and frequent replacement.

away. The loss in condition and the estimated wear rate is factored in to the quality and life expectancy of the rail. Rails that were used on main lines often saw a second lease of life on branch lines and then again in sidings, where the speeds were slower and the trains were lighter. The new rails we were putting on were actually second-hand, as they had previously been used elsewhere on Britain's rail network.

The location we were working in proved to be quite challenging. The view from the crane is limited and it requires constant vigilance to see what is going on. Not only did Keith have to concentrate on moving the load, he had to be aware of obstacles such as the mile markers on the steep bank, the trees and a bridge. Margaret worked as his 'banksman', directing his movements with hand signals that most people working on building sites today would recognize.

The crane was very quiet. Unlike a diesel crane, which has a noisy engine, the only real noise was from the movement of the pistons and the winch. When the crane was stationary it was possible for Keith to speak quite clearly to Margaret on the ground. The work ebbs and flows, which gives the crane driver time to stoke the fire and build the steam ready to trundle up and down the track and raise and lower the crane.

As each rail was put in place, the crew would see it home. They wiggled it into position in the chairs and bolted it to the last rail laid, using a fishplate. A gap for expansion is left, but modern rails are now continuous and the way the steel is produced allows for expansion and contraction within the rail itself. The rails are cut up at the manufacturing point and re-welded in situ. The first welded rails were used in the 1920s in Germany. After the Hither Green rail crash in 1967, in which 49 people lost their lives, British Rail sped up the introduction of continuous welded rail on the mainline. The crash had been caused by a crack forming at the bolt hole on the fishplate, which had gone unnoticed and had become progressively worse. Cracks at bolt holes were a common problem.

The crew tapped home the keys that wedge the rail to the chairs. The navvies building the permanent way would have laid the track by hand, using bars, jacks and shovels. It would have been hard work and they needed to get it right. The crew at Keighley also made sure that the ballast was free of weeds and in sufficient supply to do its job. The importance of ballast spreading the load, giving adequate drainage and anchoring sleepers in place cannot be over emphasized. When ballast is first laid, the gaps between the rocks, devoid of any soil, is not an environment conducive to cultivation. However, soil from leaf litter and blown from the banks builds up over time, and soon a well-drained weed bed establishes itself. The oil, steam, ash and cinders that came out of the bottom of engines often took care of any new shoots of vegetation – but not always.

If plants took root in the ballast, they could interfere with the track and badly affect drainage. Even if the track was not flooded, if the ballast became waterlogged and then froze, it could actually distort the rails, as when water freezes its volume increases by as much as nine per cent. Until the 1930s, ballast was cleared of any vegetation by hand. After this time, weedkilling trains were employed to spray the ballast. The trains would be made up of old steam engine tenders, into which water and chemicals could be placed. The liquids would be piped to the back of the train, where a brake van had spray nozzles added. The pumps worked off the axles of the vans and the required mixture of weedkiller to water could be delivered at a force of about two bar.

As we headed back to the shed to put the crane away and dispose of our now filthy rags, I thought about all the people who both built and maintained the railways. All those countless men, women and children who lived and often died working on the very trackways that we now take for granted…

OVERLEAF: The magnificent Victorian arched roof at Paddington Station, created by the legendary engineer, Isambard Kingdom Brunel.

STATION ARCHITECTURE

The permanent way connects two destinations with a number of stops along the way – but how do people access trains? The railway, in terms of trains and track, came long before stations. Instead, buildings that already existed – such as cowsheds and wooden barns – were used as makeshift passenger pens. Sometimes engines were stored in these locations as well, and it was not uncommon for the barns to burn down. Public houses were also frequently used as places to gather passengers and issue tickets.

The term booking hall – which we still use today – is adopted from the old coaching practice of issuing tickets from a book. These tickets were handwritten and the process was laborious. A stationmaster and trained cabinet-maker named Thomas Edmondson introduced the Edmondson railway ticket in 1837 (*see* page 182). These pre-printed tickets were all uniquely numbered and were stamped by a machine upon issue. The system was adopted in 1842 with the introduction of the Railway Clearing House, which was a central body that could allocate a share in revenue from tickets issued for journeys that used more than one company's line. The last Edmondson ticket was issued in 1990.

Presenter Ruth Goodman buying old-style railway tickets in a period booking hall on the Bluebell Railway.

The first station to have two platforms that were distinctly for arrivals and departures was Euston station in London. All the stations along the London and Greenwich Railway are elevated, because the track was entirely built on arches. Stations had to be built to serve a function, and often their form reflected either the practicalities required to facilitate the movement of passengers or the limitations imposed by the surrounding terrain and landscape.

However, train companies realized quite quickly that their stations were beacons for their companies, as well as a statement to the passenger that they had arrived. Decorations were included in the cast iron that decorated these buildings, often doubling as practical items such as brackets. If you look at the Victorian ceiling of Paddington station, you will notice numerous stars and moons cut out of the iron, which serve both to lighten the material and provide anchor points.

An arched iron roof such as that found at Paddington station truly represents the best of Victorian engineering. Isambard Kingdom Brunel, who constructed Paddington with his associate, the architect Matthew Digby Wyatt, adopted the system for creating the roof from advancements that had been made by Joseph Paxton. Paxton was an architect and a gardener, and while working at Chatsworth House he designed and built a series of greenhouses, each more elaborate than the last. They were engineered to provide maximum light and their ridge and furrow roofs allowed for good drainage. In these structures he cultivated the Cavendish banana, which is now the most consumed type of banana in the world.

Paxton's largest greenhouse was the Great Conservatory, which would act as a prototype for his most famous creation (other than the aforementioned banana) – the Crystal Palace. Crystal Palace was constructed in Hyde Park in 1851, from prefabricated cast iron and glass, before being moved to Sydenham, where it was destroyed by fire in 1936. This, along with Burton's Palm house at Kew, opened the floodgates for station architecture.

Built in 1854, the same year as Paddington station, Birmingham New Street station held the record for the widest roof span at 64 metres. However, this would not last long. London, Glasgow and Belfast all saw stations with amazing arched roofs being built. Then, in 1868 St Pancras station was constructed – with a huge roof coming in at a staggering 74 metres. This roof was different – it had no struts or ties, because it used a latticed arch. When St Pancras was recently renovated, the colour of the underlying paint was discovered and reinstated – a beautiful sky blue.

Euston station's classical Doric arch was a highlight of Victorian architecture.

St Pancras is also the proud possessor of another great example of Victorian station features – the grand entrance. Designed by Sir George Gilbert Scott and comprising of both booking hall and hotel, St Pancras is stunning in all its gothic revival glory. The arched windows are accentuated by red and white sunbursts and the building is constructed from all the main bedrocks that the railway's permanent way traverses.

Another station that was given a fabulous entrance was Euston. However, sadly Euston station's classic Doric arch was destroyed in the 1960s, prompting a campaign to save St Pancras from a similar fate. Once described as the 'gateway to the north', all that is left of the entrance today are the gatehouses – now bars – that are emblazoned with all the original destinations of the railway.

Although big engine halls were in vogue for terminus stations in the nineteenth century, they were hugely expensive, so lesser stations along the line had to settle instead for platform awnings. The awnings often featured an ornate wooden valance, which was a style that quickly spread throughout the world. However, from the very first stations to the most recent stations, collectively they represent a wealth of architectural styles. This is a constant reminder that the railways are always changing – and of the incalculable influence that they have had on a global scale.

The stately Victorian entrance to St Pancras station and hotel.

CHAPTER 3

AGRICULTURE

The relationship between agriculture and railways has always been complicated. However, it has also been extremely influential in many areas of British life – no more so than during the nineteenth century.

To begin with, in order to get the railways started, there was the simple business of land ownership. The companies that wanted to construct the railways were obliged to undertake the purchase of a quite substantial acreage of land, spread in thin strips across the countryside. To those who owned the land, this proved to be a thoroughly lucrative development. Opposition to the railways was regularly countered by the companies that built them paying over the odds for disputed lands. Offers of around four times the market value were not uncommon at the time.

However, those who worked and lived off the land had a rather different outlook from the eagerly selling owners. '*The proposed line will also be very injurious to the land generally, particularly as it is upon an embankment (some of the fields will be divided into small triangular pieces)*', worried Joseph Hull. The majority of people who actually farmed the land were not owners but tenants, renting a patch from someone else. Little of the cash involved in the purchase for railway building was likely to come their way; instead, they had to deal with the inevitable disruption caused by construction and work out a way to cope with having their smallholding arbitrarily chopped in two. How were these tenants to move carts and livestock between areas of the farm with a railway running between the farmstead and fields? And how were they to cultivate those odd little strips and corners that were too small for farm machinery to access properly? Farmers were also worried about drainage and water supplies. New railway cuttings and embankments were liable to cause flooding in some areas and pond drying in others. This made some land too boggy to farm and denied livestock water in other places.

The voices that were most often and loudly raised in opposition to the coming of the railways were those of the aristocracy, simply because they were the people most able to get their voices heard. For example, the wealthy landowner Lord Harborough was adamant that the railway should not cross his estate at Stapleford Park in Leicestershire. George Stephenson proposed a route for a railway between Peterborough and Syston that ran directly through the park. However, Lord Harborough refused to sell the land and sent his estate workers out to keep the surveyors off the property. The Midland railway men were accustomed to

The Britain that the early railways literally invaded was a bucolic, peaceful place with centuries-old traditions. In the 1830s, most parts remained largely untouched by the effects of the burgeoning agricultural and industrial revolutions.

local hostility and not above a bit of trespass. Once an Act of Parliament for a proposed route had been passed, the land could be compulsorily purchased. However, there could be no Act of Parliament passed until that land had been surveyed and shown to be fit for purpose, so this was the moment at which most arguments erupted. Stakes were high for all concerned and tempers flew. In the confusion at Stapleford Park, surveying equipment was broken, fists flew and one of the surveyors even drew a gun. The local press dubbed it 'The Battle of Saxby' and the railway men, especially the trigger-happy surveyor, were lucky to spend no more than a few days in gaol. Lord Harborough was an influential man and in the end the railway company was forced to admit defeat, resulting in the line being constructed in a great loop around his estate. However, few other dissenting landowners were able to have such an effect on the way that the railways were constructed.

THE BENEFITS OF THE NEW TECHNOLOGY

Despite the early disagreements, once the first railway lines were established many farmers proved to be very forward looking, becoming modern businessmen who were eager to exploit the new technology. The initial benefit that the railways brought was the ease with which livestock could now be taken to market. For large-scale concerns producing animals for meat, the additional profits to be made as a result of rail transport were initially very good indeed. London in particular drew its meat from all corners of the country. The Highlands of Scotland and the hills and mountains of Wales produced small sturdy, high-quality beef cattle that were walked right across the country along drove roads into the centre of London, where they were sold and slaughtered. Stretches of drove road can still be identified, as much by pub names as by the physical remains of these routes, that radiate out from London to the upland pastures. Look out for old roads with very wide verges and very substantial boundaries. Old droving routes are often a little sunken into the surrounding countryside, with sturdy banks and hedges at either side. They often feature dogleg turns as well, creating sheltered spaces out of the worst of the rain and snow.

Sheep were also moved across the countryside from hillsides to markets, and even poultry was walked to its final destination. Daniel Defoe reported that 150,000 turkeys made the annual journey from East Anglia to London on foot, taking about three months to do so, and Nottingham still has a Goose Fair dating back to the annual march of birds destined for the table at the end of autumn. Such trading and agricultural habits stretched back far into the country's past, but in the late eighteenth and early nineteenth centuries – following vast population expansion in the towns and cities – the meat market was booming. Improved husbandry methods developed during the agricultural revolution allowed farmers to meet this increased demand, so the numbers of animals on the move across the country had grown hugely. The sight of large herds walking by was a regular feature of town and country life, the animals tended by a robust bunch of men and boys who were skilled not just

> "SHEEP WERE ALSO MOVED ACROSS THE COUNTRYSIDE FROM HILLSIDES TO MARKETS, AND EVEN POULTRY WAS WALKED TO ITS FINAL DESTINATION."

PREVIOUS PAGES: Many of the early railways literally drove a wedge straight through the heart of the British countryside.

The droving of livestock of all kinds had been a feature of country life in many parts of the world for centuries. The railways were to change that practice, first in Britain and then beyond.

in managing livestock, but in handling cash and negotiations. Accounts of herds taking an hour to pass by and of flocks stretching for half a mile along the road are not uncommon. Dogs ran alongside the men and livestock, keeping the herds on the move. The Welsh drovers were particularly reliant upon corgis. Brave and agile, they were not intimidated by the black cattle but would dart in and nip at their heels if the beasts were reluctant to leave a particularly good patch of grass. The men were all licensed. Regulations dating back to Tudor times insisted that each man was a married homeowner of thirty years of age or more, as a guarantee that he would be no feckless drifter but instead a reliable and responsible protector of the valuable livestock. He was also exempted from the Disarming Acts of 1716 and 1748, meaning that he was free to carry weapons. Drovers needed arms because they carried a lot of money, particularly on return journeys.

There were a couple of inherent problems with the old droving system, however – problems that the railways could and did address. It took a long time to walk beasts the length and breadth of the nation at between only six and twelve miles per day, and invariably the animals were not in a very good state when they arrived at their destination. The lengthy timescale involved in droving tied up everyone's money, delaying

An early cattle truck from the Great Western Railway, carefully restored to something approaching its original condition.

Presenter Ruth Goodman reflecting on the incalculable effect that the early railways had on the British countryside and then across the world at large.

the eventual sale of the livestock, while animals that had been in the best condition were invariably much leaner and lighter in weight when they finally did make it to market. Of course, come sale time this meant that they were therefore less valuable. Naturally, a good drover walked the animals slowly and arranged the best grazing he could for them en route in order to minimize the problem, but still it remained. Loading beasts onto a wagon and carrying them from farm to market was clearly much quicker and kept the weight on the animals. Early estimates of the financial advantage are enormous. '*I consider it to be an essential service to myself and the farmers on the line; had it passed ten or 15 years ago it would have been a benefit to me of not less than £50 per annum.*' Thus opined a man with 400 acres next to a proposed line in Oxfordshire. Naturally, such profits did not hold true for long – the price of good fat stock quickly fell. However, it was that fall in price in turn that made the old droving system even more uneconomical.

Where the railways went, the droving business collapsed, almost at an instant. For example, in 1845 the Bird in Hand public house at Tasburgh in Norfolk was a temporary way station for 9,300 beasts; however, a year later only twelve animals were grazed there overnight. Livestock was clearly a major source of business for the railways from day one. Nor

was the flow of animals confined to London – other towns and cities attracted their own meat trade and there was also a new upsurge in the livestock fattening trade. Sheep and cattle raised on high pastures had traditionally been moved on down to lower-lying, richer pastures, where they could grow fat. Railway transport not only increased the numbers of animals being moved for this purpose, but also increased the distances that were possible between the two locations. New patterns of livestock movement began to become established. Cattle trucks were to become one of the earliest and most widespread forms of railway vehicle and few rural stations existed without livestock loading ramps. For forty years, the livestock farmers of Britain were among the railway's most ardent fans.

INTERNATIONAL SUCCESS

Meanwhile, the considerable advantages of the railway were being discovered by another group of farmers halfway around the world.

The forging of the railroad across the plains of America is one of the most iconic images of the 'Wild West'. The United States was among the very first nations to follow the British lead and build railways – indeed,

The driving of the Golden Spike, joining the Central Pacific and Union Pacific railroads to complete the first transcontinental railroad across the United States. This seminal event took place on 10 May 1869, at Promontory Summit, Utah Territory.

The American cowboy of legend was soon largely to become a thing of the past, once the railways had a foothold across the United States.

British expertise, engineering and finance were to heavily underpin the first phase of American rail endeavours.

The American soils had proved fertile and productive, yet the population on the land was still comparatively small, particularly away from the east coast. A tradition of agricultural regions in the west producing large surpluses that were transported huge distances back east was well established by the time the Golden Spike was driven into place in 1869, connecting the east and west of the great nation by rail. The cattle ranchers had set the pattern decades before, with cowboys driving the steers back east. The new railways cut short these epic journeys down to size, but across the huge open landscape of the United States, shorter cattle drives continued bringing the animals to the nearest railway for several decades after the great cross-continent drives ceased. If railways limited the role of cowboys, they profited the ranchers themselves, much as they did for British livestock farmers – speeding up transport and raising the value of their beasts at market. With more opportunities for making a good living, cattle farming in America actually increased as the cowboys faded away. Grain farming was much more dependent on close proximity to the railways for transport to market, and for a while it was possible to map the land use of America simply by looking at where the

railway lines ran. Wheat followed one or two years behind the expanding lines, as they continued to push out into new territory.

The American railways and the agriculture that they supported were quickly to become well established and the flows of produce thoroughly embedded. What was needed now was a new market for the steadily increasing surpluses pouring eastwards. Populations in the cities were rising fast, but still there was plenty of produce to spare. Enter the steam ship. These craft had been around for a while, initially operating on inland waterways and then tentatively out across the open ocean. The first purpose-built steam ship intended for regular transatlantic trade was the brainchild of Isambard Kingdom Brunel, the same engineer who created the Great Western Railway. Indeed, it was his stated intention to create a cross-Atlantic business that continued on from that railway. Brunel's first ship, the *SS Great Western*, put to sea in 1838. It could power across the Atlantic in faster times through heavier seas with larger cargos than anything that had gone before. One crossing that year was achieved in fourteen days and seven hours. Brunel followed it with more and even bigger ships and his competitors did likewise. Larger, faster ships meant that bigger cargoes were possible at lower costs per ton. Bulk transportation was entering a new era across sea as well as land.

The rapidly constructed American railroads of the mid-nineteenth century reduced the size of the vast continent and revolutionized the export of wheat and other produce.

Isambard Kingdom Brunel's fast and robust **SS** *Great Western* **was a hugely important innovation in terms of linking the railways with the transcontinental export trade.**

Cheap American wheat from the vast plains began arriving in bulk at British ports, to be offloaded onto another set of trains and carried direct to the urban population of late Victorian Britain. A trickle at first, by the 1880s the imports had become a flood. Argentinian beef, again transported overland by rail, was not far behind, with New Zealand lamb hot on its tail. These innovations were a huge boost to the labouring people of Britain's industrial heartlands, offering far more inexpensive basic food. The 1840s in particular had seen widespread food shortages, but now there was more to go around and whole new sectors of the urban working classes could eat meat on a regular basis.

However, the picture was far less rosy out on the land. Disastrously undercut by the huge volumes of cheap imports of both meat and grain, British farming went into a severe and lasting depression.

"CHEAP **AMERICAN WHEAT** FROM THE VAST PLAINS BEGAN ARRIVING IN **BULK** AT BRITISH PORTS, TO BE OFFLOADED ONTO ANOTHER **SET OF TRAINS.**"

CATTLE WAGONS

The first cattle to be moved by rail were transported in much the same carriages used by third-class passengers, although without the wooden benches. Low-sided, wooden-floored open wagons with four wheels bumped and trundled along, with the cattle standing exposed to all weathers. These carriages were in truth more all-purpose wagons rather than cattle wagons, but it was soon recognized that just as third-class passengers should be provided with a roof and some shelter from the rain, so too should cattle. The increasing speeds of trains played a part in this realization. Typical goods train speeds of under ten miles per hour had generally been considered reasonable in the 1840s, but by 1860 even goods trains were regularly operating at twenty or thirty miles per hour, over certain stretches of line. The cattle were suffering and losing condition as a result. The new roofed and walled cattle wagons that began to come into service were equipped with a big gap at the top of the wall, just beneath the roof, to ensure ample ventilation. They also featured a moveable partition that farmers could use to separate beasts and prevent them from hurting themselves while in transit. The new wagon design turned out to be so useful for a host of other purposes that this became the primary pattern for goods vans in general. Many of them were converted by the simple expedient of filling in the ventilation gap with a few additional slats.

What the railway had given, the railway had taken away…. In the 1880s, after that first forty years of plenty, British agriculture had to come to terms with the fact that the globalization the railways brought meant change. The honeymoon was over: British farmers would have to dig deep and find a new way of working with rail.

MILK

Milk was one commodity that witnessed enormous railway-driven expansion in terms of its availability and popularity during the nineteenth century. However, the story around this product is also one of the tragic spread of disease and the decline of the traditional cheese industry. The promotion of milk was at the forefront of one farmer's mind as early as 1839.

'I have been a dairyman 20 years and have 40 or 50 cows, and I consider that a railway would be still more important to the dairy farmers, as they would be able to send milk and butter to the London Market. I had offers made to me to supply a part of London with milk, but I could not for want of conveyance;

if we could get a railroad we should increase the profits 400 or 500 per cent on milk and butter.' (W. Meade Warner)

Four to five hundred per cent profits were very wishful thinking on Mr Warner's part, but in essence his thinking was correct.

A regular supply of fresh milk from the countryside began to be transported along railway lines into Manchester in 1844 and to London a year later. When the Eastern Counties Railway started to regularly carry fresh milk from Brentford and Romford in Essex overnight into London, they tried to do so using traditional milk pails. These had been used by milkmaids for centuries, and were designed to be carried across the women's shoulders upon yokes. Carrying the same pails by rail proved

The traditional yoke-bearing milkmaid had been a staple of British country life for centuries. However, this was yet another means of trade that died with the advent of the railways.

to be not terribly successful. The pails were too top heavy to cope with the often bumpy journey and frequently toppled over, spilling the milk in transit. Butter churns proved much more stable. These were tall wooden casks with straight sides that tapered towards the top. They were much larger with a greater capacity than the pails, but easier to manoeuvre if they were rolled on their base rims. Of course, the early ones were really butter-making churns, made out of wooden staves bound together with iron bands. Within a few years, however, a separate purpose-built metal version was introduced, designed purely for transporting milk. The name 'churn' was retained, though. Some of these new churns were made of iron with a coating of tin inside, some were brass, and most had some sort of identifying stamp or label to say which dairy they belonged to. Safely contained, the fresh milk made its way into the big towns and cities – but there were still a number of problems. The biggest issue arose from the speed and ride quality of the journey. Small four-wheeled wagons moving across short lengths of jointed track were constantly shaking the milk in the churns so that it arrived denatured and homogenized. On hot days, it might also be sour by the time it arrived at its destination. Many potential customers turned their noses up at railway milk, instead

PREVIOUS PAGES: Historians Peter Ginn, Ruth Goodman and Alex Langlands standing aboard a train on the Foxfields Railway near Stoke-on-Trent.

Early milk churns were big, heavy and incredibly unwieldy. However, they were also stable and kept the milk relatively cool.

preferring that which came from cows kept within the city.

Even London was well provided with its own herds of cows, fed largely upon hay and other fodder brought into the city from the countryside

"IN 1865, DISASTER STRUCK LONDON'S HERDS. A FATAL BOVINE DISEASE NAMED 'RINDERPEST' SWEPT THROUGH THE CAPITAL, DESTROYING CATTLE."

around and kept in a network of small open spaces and even in basements. These urban animals provided genuinely fresh milk, even if the dubious health of the cows meant that it was of rather poor quality. In 1850 less than five per cent of London's milk was brought in by rail, about fifteen per cent came in on the back of a cart from the surrounding countryside and the rest – a full eighty per cent – was produced within the city. However, new scientific investigations were beginning to challenge this state of affairs. Work upon the nature of nutrition and the composition of food was beginning to make people question where their food was coming from. Then, in 1865, disaster struck London's herds. A fatal bovine disease named 'rinderpest' swept through the capital, destroying more than three-quarters of the cattle. Traditional supply lines were in tatters and public confidence in the supply of town milk took a serious knock. Ready and waiting were men like George Mander Allender, who were already working with a number of farmers and railway companies. In 1866, Allender founded the Aylesbury Dairy Company, with headquarters in Bayswater. He had been a dairy farmer himself, with holdings just outside Aylesbury in the village of Quainton, and at the small nearby town of Winslow. He had excellent contacts in an area of heavy clay soils that were suitable for milk production, an interest in scientific hygienic milk production, and the necessary capital to expand. Allender entered into a series of contracts with local farmers to buy their milk and transport it by rail into the capital. He insisted that those he was in business with followed the latest hygienic practices and set up a system of regular farm inspections to ensure that they did so. The Aylesbury Dairy Company gained a reputation for the high quality and purity of its milk and expanded rapidly.

The 1870s saw the introduction of two new methods of combating the problem of milk souring in transit. When the milk was treated with one of these methods, it had a longer shelf life, making its collection, transportation and delivery a less financially risky business. With the longer life that the new processes endowed, treated milk could travel greater distances from farm to doorstep. One method was an early refrigeration process (or, more accurately, a rapid cooling process) that became available in 1872. George Mander Allender was quick to re-write his contracts with his suppliers, inserting a clause insisting

The Aylesbury Dairy Company regrettably proved to be a short-lived business when George Mander Allender, on holiday in Monte Carlo enjoying the fruits of his business success, was horribly murdered in a mugging that went tragically wrong.

upon the use of the new technology. The second method, and one that the Aylesbury Dairy Company was loudly vocal in shunning, was the use of chemical additives. Commercially produced milk additives were sold to farmers and dairymen that masked or slowed the onset of souring. One was based upon boric acid, another upon a mixture of sodium nitrate and formaldehyde, and a third upon formic acid and glucose.

Both these new methods of milk preservation had a hand in expanding the market for railway milk and making large commercial dairies profitable.

By the 1880s, the dairy industry in much of Britain had been completely transformed by railway transport and, in their turn, the railways were finally beginning to be shaped by the needs of the dairy industry. The quantity of milk being transported had increased more than fifty-fold since the outbreak of rinderpest, with one farmer alone sending 19,000 gallons a year into the heart of Birmingham. From being a small add-on business, the railway companies now began to see milk as a major and highly profitable money earner. The distance that it made commercial sense to dispatch milk was also increasing, involving more and more farmers and small country stations in supplying the urban populations with fresh milk. What had begun as local transportation over distances of twenty or thirty miles was now spreading out, particularly across the more remote western parts of Britain. Meanwhile, as more milk arrived in the cities, prices dropped and the urban populations were beginning to look upon milk as a staple rather than as a luxury food. This development further increased the demand for more fresh countryside milk.

Early milk transportation had consisted of simply loading churns into any available wagon and attaching that wagon to a handy passenger service. However, as the volumes of milk being transported rose, dedicated wagons and services began to make an appearance. The first purpose-built milk van emerged in 1870 for the Great Western Railway,

OPPOSITE: **Presenter Alex Langlands climbing onto the footplate of an old green steam engine that used to carry milk on the railways.**

OVERLEAF: **A preserved steam locomotive running along the South Devon Railway, one of the main routes of early milk conveyance to the British public.**

with open-slatted sides to help the milk stay cool and six wheels rather than the more usual four, to deliver a smoother ride. The GWR in particular was beginning to schedule early morning express dairy runs.

The South Devon Railway was a typical rural branch line that opened in 1872. It runs along the valley of the river Dart, linking Buckfastleigh and Totnes to the main Great Western network. It never made a profit, but it did allow many local farmers to make a living. Early morning movements of churns became one of the most common local sights. As the cows returned to the pastures after morning milking, the farm hands strained the milk through fine meshes into the milk cooler. Cold running water from the well or local stream was played over the outer surfaces, reducing the temperature of the milk from blood heat down to around five or six degrees. The chilled liquid was then transferred into clean metal transport churns, which had to be manhandled across the farmyard to the roadside and up a series of steps onto a small platform, or stand. Each farm had one at its gate and it was from here that the delivery cart, whose flat bed was at precisely the same height as the stand, would pick them up. Milk-laden carts from all directions would begin to converge upon the station. The churns, with a capacity of seventeen gallons, were very heavy. A handle on each side allowed two men to lift one when necessary, but generally they were rolled along on their bottom rims by one man, with a distinctive rattling noise ringing out across the platform as they went. The churns, off-loaded from the carts, were organized upon the platform before the wagons pulled in. A standard milk van could take around sixty churns in a single layer. It was technically possible to double-stack the churns, but it was both slow and heavy work to do so and, with speed being of the essence, it usually made more sense simply to use more wagons. Off went the loaded wagons to join up with the others. 'Milk run' soon became an established term in the English language, describing a regular railway run that took place so early in the day that it did not suffer from the vagaries of passenger train timetabling.

Before the railway made its iron way up the Dart valley, much of the locally produced milk had been made into cheese. However, the arrival of the South Devon Railway coincided with a national slump in wholesale cheese prices, as imported factory-produced cheese flooded the British market. Liquid milk was not a highly profitable product in itself, but it was much cheaper to produce, requiring far less skilled labour and less equipment. It also offered the advantage of a quick sale, whereas cheese takes time to make, locking up capital. So, a new outlet for liquid milk must have been something of a lifesaver for hard-pressed farmers along the valley, and local artisanal cheese-making traditions quietly withered away.

As the twentieth century dawned, branch lines criss-crossing the countryside rang with the sounds of the morning milk and stations in towns and cities had their platforms submerged beneath a tide of churns that rose and fell daily. The arriving milk was handled by a host of different dairy businesses, some of which were very large indeed. Express Dairies (the word 'express' in its name being a direct reference to railway transport), United Dairies and the Co-operative Society were among those handling the largest volumes. Deliveries were made from lightweight hand- or horse-drawn carts called milk floats, which carried a large can or churn of milk and a number of measuring jugs. Customers were expected to bring their own jugs to carry the milk home in after the milkman had measured out a portion from the churn. However, at this time there were also a few pre-filled milk bottles beginning to reach the market. Express Dairies was among the first to trial this new method of sales. Like many of the big concerns, they were experimenting with heat-treating the milk, primarily as a means of extending shelf life. They sold it as 'pasteurised' milk, named after the process invented by the French scientist, Louis Pasteur. It was not particularly popular.

Raw milk straight from the cow is capable of carrying a range of diseases, from salmonella to diphtheria. However, perhaps the biggest killer lurking in early twentieth century raw milk was bovine tuberculosis. It is estimated that between 1912 and 1937 in England and Wales, sixty-five thousand people died as a direct result of drinking milk contaminated with tuberculosis.

Back in 1856, Louis Pasteur was working upon what then was considered to be a chemical problem, fermentation. Everyone within the wine and beer industry knew that the line between producing wine and 'vinegar' was a very fine one. What was it that suddenly turned a whole batch from one to the other? Pasteur was the man to discover that, rather than being the results of a purely chemical process, yeasts were real, living creatures. Following this key insight, Pasteur found

"PASTEUR WAS THE MAN TO DISCOVER THAT, RATHER THAN BEING THE RESULTS OF A PURELY CHEMICAL PROCESS, YEASTS WERE REAL, LIVING CREATURES."

OPPOSITE: The great French biologist Louis Pasteur, at work in his laboratory. His pioneering work in the mid-nineteenth century saved countless lives.

OVERLEAF: Ruth Goodman enjoying a cup of tea with milk, and Peter Ginn indulging in a bottle of beer. The purity and safety of both these drinks benefited immeasurably from the work of Louis Pasteur.

that in good alcohol the yeasts were discernible as fat round entities, but that within vinegary alcohol, there was a second, living presence of long rods that appeared to push out or kill the yeasts. After careful experimentation, he found that he could kill these long rods without damaging the flavour of the wine or beer, by applying just the right amount of heat for just the right amount of time. Pasteur patented this process and named it after himself – 'pasteurisation'. It would be this work that led him on to discover that disease in humans is caused by microscopic living creatures, one of the most important discoveries in human history.

It took a long time for Pasteur's discoveries to have an impact upon milk production. The first commercial pasteurisers, using a high heat over a short period of time, arrived on the market in 1882. It was this system that companies such as Express Dairies used for their bottled milk. However, people were highly suspicious of this innovation in milk production. It seemed 'unnatural' – surely it would destroy the goodness of the milk? Others viewed pasteurisation in the same light as the adulteration of milk with chemical preservatives – a commercial cheat that was designed only to increase profits. As vitamins were discovered for the first time, new worries emerged about the effects of interfering with natural foods. Many other people held on to an almost spiritual faith in the direct connection between man and beast. There was also, of course, the commercial consideration. It was all very well for a large-scale operation to invest in the necessary equipment to undertake pasteurisation, but smaller businesses could not afford it. At this point, the milk industry quietly divided into two. Large concerns 'pasteurised' a portion of their milk and generally kept quite quiet about the fact, while smaller businesses did not. By 1926, only one and half per cent of all the milk consumed in the United Kingdom was pasteurised. However, even the consumers of pasteurised milk from the large dairies were not in the clear. The pasteurisation process was nothing like as safe and reliable in the first half of the twentieth century as it is now. Bovine tuberculosis pathogens could and did persist in many batches of milk that had been treated.

The deaths of so many people from

> "IT WAS ALL VERY WELL FOR A **LARGE-SCALE OPERATION** TO INVEST IN THE NECESSARY **EQUIPMENT** TO UNDERTAKE **PASTEURISATION.**"

bovine tuberculosis can sadly be attributed in part to the railways. In the late 1920s, the milk business was booming – over sixty express milk trains ran daily into London upon the Great Western Railway alone, with the entire network transporting 282 million gallons of milk every year. Tankers began to replace churns. The first were lined with vitreous enamel, ran upon four-wheeled wagons and had no internal partitions. The milk tended to slosh around, making the wagons unstable. However, these problems were quickly addressed, as it was clear that tankers provided a huge efficiency saving over churns. The LNER pointed out that just seven of the 3,000-gallon tanks replaced two thousand churns with none of the fuss, manpower and delay that loading and unloading churns required. However, hidden within this new clean efficient system of tankers, there lurked a problem. Within the old churn system, the milk of a contaminated beast would spoil the milk of any other milk within that particular churn – all seventeen gallons' worth. By the same token, within the tanker system, that one unhealthy cow's milk would infect the entire three thousand gallons. It would not be until the 1950s that effective mass pasteurisation of milk stemmed the tide of tuberculosis.

The new tanker system was also to herald the end of the link between milk and rail. The tanks that sat upon the flat-bed wagons were not owned by the railway companies, but by the dairies – and nor were they necessarily permanently fixed in place. A tank loaded onto a flat-bed lorry could be driven around the farms picking up the milk, as the old horse and cart had done, before being taken to the station and loaded onto a wagon for the long distance part of the journey. This was the application of new petrol-driven technology, which once again offered improved efficiency in speeding up the loading and unloading process. This was despite the fact that early lorries travelled at much the same speeds as the old horses and carts had done. However, as lorries gradually became faster and more robust, the desire to use the railway for a portion of the journey diminished. By 1969, there were just four dedicated milk trains a day running from Devon and Cornwall into London. By this time, most milk was now being moved in lorry tankers by road.

BRANCH LINES AND WHISKY

As we have seen, the earliest railways were built for industry – for coalmines, slate quarries and ironworks. The second phase in the expansion of the railway network sought to capitalize upon passenger traffic, ferrying people in and out of our major towns and cities. The third and final great expansion of the network was more agriculturally

inspired. This was the era of branch lines, built when the main lines were more or less complete, in the later 1850s and '60s. This plethora of small lines hoped to pick up business from small-scale suppliers and producers and local communities travelling to market. Milk formed one strand of the agricultural trade of these lines, as we saw with the South Devon Railway, but there were plenty of others. For example, the Sandy and Potton Railway in Cambridgeshire opened in 1857 and was designed from the outset to carry fruit and vegetables in one direction and manure in the other. The latter part of the railway's role even included a contract to dispose of the collected dung of the London Zoo.

The Strathspey Railway Line in the highlands of Scotland was built in 1863 in the hope of attracting the business of a number of very particular agricultural producers, the whisky distilleries. Certainly there was not much in the way of high-value passenger traffic in this part of the world... In 1887, Alfred Barnard wrote '*although Carron station had been open for more than 20 years, we were the only persons who had ever booked to Cromdale first class, the number of our tickets, which were faded with age, commencing at nought.*' However, the railway line did pass close to several major whisky producers, such as the Balmenach distillery at Cromdale,

A view towards the Glenlivet distillery and Blairfindy Castle in the highlands of Scotland.

The celebrated Scottish poet Robert 'Rabbie' Burns, who at one time was a customs official and scourge of the illicit whisky trade in Scotland.

as well as the Dailuaine, Cardhu, Glen Grant, Glen Farcas and Macallan distilleries.

Among the oldest in Scotland, the Balmenach distillery was officially founded in 1824, following on from the 1823 Excise Act. However, it is more than likely that the business was in full swing – albeit outside the law – well before that. Distilled alcohol, known as *aqua vita* in Latin, the 'water of life' in English and *Uisge Beatha* or *Usquebaugh* in Gaelic is recorded in Scotland from 1494, and the name was already being shortened to *Uiskie* (whisky) by 1618. The drink became subject to taxation not long after that. Perhaps understandably, the Scots did not take too kindly to having to pay tax on their home-produced whisky. This was a feeling that intensified after the 1707 Act of Union with England, when a newly efficient set of outsiders tried to collect the tax – and at a higher rate, as well. Secretly produced whisky was moved about the countryside in the hands of smugglers pursued by customs officials (of whom the famous poet Robert Burns was one). In 1820, roughly half of all the whisky consumed in Scotland had evaded the excise officers, and that was despite that fact that the customs officers were confiscating something in the region of 14,000 stills each year. The 1823 Act finally adopted a more sensible approach, offering licenses for £10 a year for anyone producing over forty gallons of whisky, dropping the duty upon the alcohol substantially, and making production at a smaller scale wholly illegal. This arrangement was much easier to enforce and considerably more affordable for the producers. As a consequence, within a decade the centuries-old tradition of whisky smuggling had fizzled out.

The MacGregor family of Balmenach had a longstanding reputation as illicit whisky producers and had suffered from a customs raid not long before the law changed. The raiders had discovered and destroyed a still in a cavern several hundred yards from where the new legal distillery now stands. One of the reasons that illicit production had been so easy to organize, and presumably the reason that the MacGregor family were so quickly able to set up a full-scale distillery after the rules changed, was the fact that the early and bulky stages of whisky production are identical to that of beer production. Home-brewed beer was a respectable staple, and not subject to the same taxation, so the large-scale buildings and equipment required could be openly set up and used. It was a fairly simple matter to take some barrels of this legally brewed beer off to a small secret location for the final distillation process that turned it into whisky. It was also not that hard to hide the resultant liquor amongst barrels of beer back at the main farmhouse. In 1824, all that the MacGregors had to do in order to convert to an immediate semblance of respectability was to relocate this section of the process somewhere more convenient alongside the rest of their brewing paraphernalia.

Over at Cardhu, Mr Cumming and his wife Helen had much the same story to tell, with Mrs Cumming in particular having a history of

Today, the manufacturing of whisky is big business, featuring a wide range of sophisticated equipment. However, its origins as a cottage industry were altogether simpler.

The barrels used to hold and transport whisky have always been very similar to those used in beer production. This meant that some illegal output could easily be hidden from the predatory customs officers.

OVERLEAF: Presenter Peter Ginn delivering barrels of beer to a pub in Matlock, Derbyshire.

welcoming the visiting customs men into her home and then secretly raising a red flag to let the neighbours know. The Cummings' whisky output, too, became a legitimate business in 1824.

Whisky production traditionally began with soaking the barley in water for around three days to encourage germination and then killing off the shoots with hot air and smoke. Both the MacGregors and the Cummings used peat fires to do this, imparting a strong flavour to the resultant whisky. Once dry, the malted barley was coarsely ground and put into a great mash tub where hot water was added; the tub at the MacGregors' farm was fourteen feet across and four feet deep and made of wooden staves. The hot mash was stirred with large wooden paddles to release all the sugars from the malt. Three separate tub-fulls of water went into each batch of malt. When the water was drawn off, it went into a series of smaller 'wash vats', where it was first cooled, and then the yeast was added. The 'wash' stayed here for up to five days as the yeast got to work, turning the sweet liquid into beer. The newly relocated stills received this beer, where it was boiled. The alcohol was boiled off, and the vapour was captured and condensed back into liquid alcohol. At this stage of the procedure, the mixture was called 'low wine'. A second distillation made it even stronger, with an alcohol content of between

sixty and seventy per cent. This 'new make' whisky could then be put into barrels to age.

The market for the newly legal spirit broadened after 1831, when Aeneas Coffey invented a new type of still which enabled a continuous process of distillation that not only speeded up production but allowed a milder smoother form of whisky to be made, using a mixture of malted and unmalted grain. This new 'grain whisky' made a drink that had a much wider appeal, particularly when blended with the traditional 'malt whiskies', converting many people over to whisky drinking.

Other elements of modernization were also creeping in. The Dailuaine distillery near Carron was founded a few years later, at some time around 1851 – no one is precisely sure of the date. It benefited from a number of instances of mechanization, with a continuous screw transporting the barley from granary to malting house and a patented sieving machine that cleaned the barley of all the bits of gravel and other detritus that might have got mixed in by accident. The kiln floor upon which the sprouted barley was dried in the rising hot air and peat smoke was made of perforated iron. The mash tub was also a much more up to date model than those mentioned before, being fitted with a brass-paddled stirring machine. All such refinements allowed the distillers to increase their outputs.

The distilleries up and down the Spey valley were now bringing in large quantities of barley from outside to satisfy demand and sending out large volumes of finished whisky – all by horse and cart, across difficult terrain. This was the type of business that the railway hoped to capture. It proved to be a good marriage, and in the way of these things soon attracted even more trade. With a railway line to ease the transport issues, whisky distilling in the Spey Valley looked like an increasingly attractive prospect, which tempted a number of other people to set up business in the area. One of these new, railway-inspired distilleries was that at Cragganmore, founded in 1869, six years after the line opened. It was set up by James Smith, who had worked as the general manager at the Macallen, Glenlivet and Wishow distilleries, leasing land from Sir

> **"THE NEW GRAIN WHISKY MADE A DRINK THAT HAD A MUCH WIDER APPEAL, PARTICULARLY WHEN BLENDED WITH THE TRADITIONAL MALTS."**

COOPERING AND DISTILLING

Strathspey is an area in the northwest of Scotland that is famous for its single malt whiskies. Much of the industry owes its growth and global success to the railways, which both brought in raw materials and carried out the finished product. Today, the distilleries are experiencing an increase in demand, with new distilleries such as the one at Ballindalloch opening up.

Whisky is first brewed like a beer and is then passed through the stills, which boil the liquid and condense the alcohol. The spirit that is collected is clear like vodka, and cannot be classed as Scotch whisky for three years. During this time the spirit is put into wooden casks and stored in a Scottish warehouse. It is the cask that gives whisky its colour and much of its flavour. This makes the cooper's job very important.

There are a number of cooperages in Scotland and demand for casks is high. One of the largest is the Speyside cooperage in Craigellachie. In the yard there are about 150,000 casks piled into pyramidical structures that have come from all over the world. Although coopers make casks of varying sizes and for a variety of reasons – including serving as pistons on the very first steam engines – for distilleries it is the cask's past life that creates the future whisky.

The Speyside cooperage is a hive of activity. Everyone working on the floor engaged in the ancient art of coopering is on 'piece' work, which means their pay is directly linked to their output. The casks in the yard are lined up in rows in a collection area and each cooper takes the next one in line. This is the fairest way to divide the casks out over time, as some need very little attention and others quite a lot.

The cooper moves the cask by a process known as 'chiming'. This involves tipping the casks onto its chime or its rim and rolling it while keeping it balanced. Some of these coopers could chime a cask faster than I could walk! The cask is then scrubbed with a wire brush and any staves that are damaged are marked with chalk. The broken wood is removed

and a new piece is planed down to match each of the neighbouring staves, and cut to fit the length of the cask. There are no nails, no glue and the only 'joints' are the grooves that are cut at either end of the cask in order to take the heads or the ends. These grooves are packed with either dried straw or water reed.

The whole container is held together by metal hoops. A large cask of wine from Gaul was found recently in London some 1,800 years after it was buried in a well. It has metal hoops similar to those that are used today. However, some casks were made with hazel hoops – especially if they contained gunpowder – as the metal hoops could create sparks when the casks were moved. The hazel was beneficial as it was more appealing to insects than the seasoned oak, meaning that the casks would remain protected for longer.

Once a cask has been made good, the cooper then chars it. In the past this was done over a small fire, but now it is done over controllable gas jets. The charring of the inside of the cask is intended to open up the tight grain of the oak staves and is done to a special, individual level dictated by each of the distilleries. This allows the previous contents of the cask – be it sherry, port, wine or bourbon – to mix with the clear spirit over time and create what we know as whisky.

George Macpherson Grant up at Ballindalloch Castle. Smith chose that particular spot for its combination of good water supplies and proximity to the line itself, asking for, and getting, a new private station for the works. John Smith clearly liked railways, for he begged a ride on the footplate – although when he found that he did not quite fit the small driving space, he had to settle for a ride in the guard's van.

The 1880s saw another jump in whisky sales, as disaster struck the wine industry in France. Phylloxera beetle rampaged through the ancient vineyards of Europe and struck France particularly badly. Almost the entire French wine industry was significantly affected. Export supplies of wine and brandy dried up, and into this vacuum canny distillery owners promoted their own products vigorously. By the time the French winegrowers began to recover, a taste for Scottish whisky had become well established all across Britain.

In 1887, on the back of this rise in sales, the first of a series of 'whisky specials' made its way out of the station at Cragganmore bound for Aberdeen, pulling twenty-five wagons loaded with three hundred casks of liqour. Following Cragganmore's lead, some of the older established distilleries began to improve their connections to the railway. Both Dailuaine and Balmenach had been content to take their whisky by cart to the stations, but now they invested in small tramways directly linking their warehouses with the line, each with their own small tank engines known as 'tuggies', to pull the load.

GLOBAL VERSUS LOCAL

In agriculture perhaps more clearly than in any other area, it is possible to see the way that the railways opened up the global economy and encouraged local specialization at one and the same moment. As the railways rolled out across the landscapes of the world, they created a path for produce to roll out, as well. In that first flush, the flow was securely outward from the productive heartlands of Britain. British beef boomed, as did British iron and steel, but as things settled, new multi-directional streams of produce began to establish themselves. Global markets became more fluid and responsive, as well as more competitive. It was easy to get left behind or overwhelmed by the greater natural resources of other parts of the world. Cheap American and Canadian wheat meant cheaper, more plentiful bread for the urban workers; Argentinian beef and New Zealand lamb meant more meat upon the table than ever before. However, these new imports left the native farming community slumped deep in poverty. The more canny and

The Watercress Line at Ropley Station, Hampshire. The Cheltenham locomotive is approaching the platform.

OVERLEAF: Presenters Peter Ginn, Alex Langlands and Ruth Goodman carrying a hamper of produce at a railway station on a preserved line.

adaptable members of the rural economy responded by going local – finding products that could not be replicated globally and new markets for items that had once been specialist and restricted to certain localities.

The Mid-Hants Railway that opened in 1865 had originally been built as an alternative route across the hills to Southampton, seeking to draw business away from the established line and serve the needs of the armed forces, moving troops from Aldershot down to the port. It was never terribly successful at enticing the London to Southampton traveller, although it did move a lot of soldiers. These days, the railway is more commonly known as the Watercress Line, as this agricultural product became the major goods item to move along it. The clean, clear, chalky waters of the local rivers and streams offered the perfect environment for wild watercress. However, cultivation of the plant did not begin until the beginning of the nineteenth century, when William Bradbury devised a method of farming it and went into business near Gravesend in Kent in 1809. As a free and flavourful wild food, watercress had become a staple of working people's breakfasts wherever it grew, ideally sandwiched between two slices of bread. As rural people from these areas moved into towns, they took their taste for the plant with them,

and the new watercress farmers did their best to supply them. By 1861 Henry Mayhew was recording London street scenes, as follows:

'The first Coster cry heard of a morning in the London streets is "Fresh wo-orter-creases". Those that sell them have to be on their rounds in time for the mechanics' breakfast, or the day's gains are lost.'

Railways first gave growers in Kent and southern Hertfordshire a means of getting their produce into Covent Garden market and thence into the morning sandwiches of London's workers. The arrival of the Mid-Hants Railway opened up the London market to the growers of the Arlesford region, who had previously served only the small market towns of the surrounding region. Watercress beds were expanded and more people became involved, with large numbers of local men employed daily to pick the cresses by hand and local women to clean, bunch and pack them into wicker work 'flats', ready for transport. A very localized food had become much more widely available and it had as part of that story produced intense local pockets of agricultural specialization.

Further west, the people of the Tamar Valley on the border between Devon and Cornwall became specialist strawberry and cherry farmers. In 1862, the 22-year-old James Walter Lawry travelled up to

"SIX MILLION PEOPLE – A THIRD OF THE ENTIRE POPULATION OF BRITAIN – VISITED THE EXHIBITION. MOST OF THEM CAME ON THE RAILWAYS."

London to see the Great Exhibition at Crystal Palace. It was intended as a showcase of British engineering, manufacturing and material culture, and the organizers hoped for a large international audience. What they got was a moderate international attendance and a stupendous level of interest from within these shores. Six million people – a third of the entire population of Britain – visited the exhibition. Most of them came by rail. It was hoped that the exhibition would stimulate trade. It certainly did so in young James Walter Lawry's case, although probably not in the way that he had imagined:

'After seeing the show, having heard of Covent Garden market, my friend and I self-determined that we would rise early and visit this renowned market whilst yet business was in progress. It was early June and to my surprise, I found that there were no out-of-door grown strawberries offered, whilst at home the crop was nearly finished before we left. On enquiring the price of the hothouse fruit offered, I was staggered at the difference from that we had been receiving at Devonport. I got into conversation with a salesman named Israel, and explained that I hailed from Cornwall and was a grower of strawberries which were now practically finished, although if he would undertake the sale I would write the people at home and get them to forward a small quantity as an experiment. He promised to do his best, and I made the venture'.

For the next forty years, intensive strawberry growing became the Tamar Valley speciality, alongside the equally profitable cherry orchards. The steep slopes were terraced and dotted with packing houses full of people, for this was very labour-intensive agriculture. Fruit gardens had become the centre of the local economy and tourists flocked to the area in spring to see the cherry blossom. None of it would have been possible without the railway to carry this fresh perishable produce speedily and in volume to the large towns and cities where their customers lived. Plymouth, at

The Great Exhibition of 1862 was held at the magnificent, purpose-built Crystal Palace.

the mouth of the Tamar river, had a mainline connection to London from 1849, and by 1860 Tavistock, just to the north of the strawberry growing region, was connected by rail to that mainline. Some of the fruit went overland by horse and cart to Tavistock station, but most of it sailed down the Tamar to Plymouth by paddleboat to connect with the rails there. In 1890, a new line opened right through the heart of the region up from Plymouth, through Bere Alston and on to Tavistock. The line was intended to provide an alternative route as one railway company competed with another, but the fruit traffic was also a considerable draw. The railway maintained its own boat and staff to help customers from the Cornish side of the valley bring produce across to the station. Extra staff were taken on during the fruit harvests at each of the local stations along the line, to help load the crop onto the trains. The railway company also offered a complimentary telegraph service, alerting wholesalers in the big cities to the exact timings and loadings of each grower's consignment of produce. Fruit picked at 8am in Cornwall could be upon the afternoon tea tables of families in Bristol, Birmingham, London and even Glasgow by 4pm on the same day.

Isambard Kingdom Brunel's world famous Royal Albert railway bridge at Plymouth, crossing the river Tamar.

CHAPTER 4

COMMUNICATION

The railways were always intended to move people and produce for profit, but with those products and people moved information and ideas. The railways broadened people's horizons, not just by permitting them to travel as never before but also by speeding up older forms of communication and facilitating entirely new ones. The nation would be linked up physically and culturally, almost by accident, in ways that changed the entire political and social landscape of Britain.

Naturally, the first thoughts about railway communications were concerned with conveying information between staff about the running of trains. The very first railway lines were equipped with little in the way of points, junctions or even many engines. What did exist was managed with a combination of flags, lamps, pocket watches, messengers and memoranda. In essence, when a man sent a train off along a section of railway line, he made a note of the time of its departure. After a full ten minutes had elapsed, he could send another train along the line, warning the driver as he did so that he should proceed with caution. However, if a longer period of time elapsed between messages being sent (different stretches of line had different time intervals), then he would tell the second driver to expect a clear run. This system worked reasonably well – so long as there were not many trains on the line in question, they travelled fairly slowly and the drivers kept a sharp eye out for trouble up ahead.

Signalmen (who to begin with were known as railway policemen) were stationed at intervals along the line with their trusty watches and notebooks. In order to slightly speed up the system, they were issued with flags and lamps. These allowed the signalmen to communicate with the driver without the train actually having to stop each time it reached a signal post. If the signalman needed to stop the train, he raised both arms above his head, waved a red flag or lamp or, in extremis, attracted the train driver's attention '*by the violent waving of any object*'. '*Proceed with caution*' was signalled by raising one arm above his head, or a green flag or lamp; the '*all clear*' signal consisted of one arm being held out horizontally across the track, or a white flag or lamp. A little ditty helped everyone to remember the signals: '*White is right; Red is wrong; Green is gently go along.*'

In the early days of the railways, signalmen carried a variety of coloured flags and other paraphernalia in what was simultaneously a complicated and hazardously basic form of communication.

Before long the signalmen were assisted by a stout wooden pole driven into the ground, from which hung a painted wooden board or an arm operated by a rope or wire. The signalman could haul on the wire to change the position of the signal arm, mimicking the positions of the original hand signals. The arm could be positioned vertically, horizontally or at a forty-five degree angle. Being both larger and taller than a man, such signals could be seen over much greater distances and in conditions of poorer visibility. The idea was borrowed from the military, which had used similar devices for sending semaphore messages across battlefields. The only problem occurred when the wires broke and the signal arm dropped down into the horizontal position which, mimicking the original arm movements meaning '*line clear*', left the signalman with no way of moving the signal to the vertical '*stop*' position. Several crashes later, the meanings attributed to the positions of the signal arms were reversed, so that the horizontal dropped position now meant '*stop*' and the driver could only proceed when the signal had been positively raised or '*pulled off*'.

Regular timetabled services for passengers were governed not only by the pocket watches and notebooks of its signalmen, but by those of the railway's drivers and station staff as well. This was fairly straightforward between Liverpool and Manchester, on that first regular steam-hauled

Bradshaw's

CONTINENTAL
RAILWAY GUIDE
AND
GENERAL HANDBOOK
ILLUSTRATED
WITH LOCAL AND OTHER
MAPS
SPECIAL EDITION.
3/6

The bright red cover of an early international edition of *Bradshaw's Railway Guide*. This handy little tome became an invaluable and firm favourite among rail travellers, both in Britain and abroad, in the second half of the nineteenth century and beyond.

"IN THE NINETEENTH CENTURY, ACROSS BRITAIN, TOWNS AND CITIES SET THEIR CLOCKS TO LOCAL MEAN TIMES."

BIRMINGHAM, SUTTON COLDFIELD, AND LICHFIELD.

The timetable shown is a dense historical railway schedule for Birmingham, Sutton Coldfield and Lichfield, divided into "WEEK DAYS" (two directions) and "SUNDAYS" sections. Key legible elements are transcribed below.

WEEK DAYS

Depart — LONDON (Euston), BIRMINGHAM, Vauxhall & Duddeston, Aston, Gravelly Hill, Erdington, Chester Road, Wylde Green, SUTTON COLDFIELD (arr/dep), Four Oaks, Blake Street, Shenstone, LICHFIELD (arr), Burton-on-Trent, Derby.

Columns marked "Saturdays excepted." and "Saturdays only."

WEEK DAYS (return direction)

Derby depart, Burton-on-Trent, LICHFIELD (City), Shenstone, Blake Street, Four Oaks, SUTTON COLDFIELD (arrive/depart), Wylde Green, Chester Road, Erdington, Gravelly Hill, Aston, Vauxhall and Duddeston, BIRMINGHAM (New St.) arr, LONDON (Euston).

SUNDAYS

LONDON (Euston) dep	a.m	p.m	a.m		p.m
BIRMINGHAM (New St.)	9	0	1 0	2 35	...	5A0
Vauxhall and Duddeston	9	4	1 4	2 39	...	8 44
Aston	9	8	1 8	2 43	...	8 43
Gravelly Hill	9 12	1 12	2 47	...	8 52
Erdington	9 15	1 15	2 50	...	8 55
Chester Road	9 19	1 19	2 54	...	8 59
Wylde Green	9 25	1 25	3 0	...	9 5
SUTTON COLDFIELD ar	9 29	1 29	3 4	...	9 9

SUNDAYS				
SUTTON COLDFIELD dp	9 40	1 50	5 40	...	9 20
Wylde Green	9 44	1 54	5 44	...	9 24
Chester Road	9 47	1 57	5 47	...	9 27
Erdington	9 50	2 0	5 50	...	9 30
Gravelly Hill	9 53	2 3	5 53	...	9 33
Aston	9 58	2 8	5 58	...	9 38
Vauxhall and Duddeston	10 3	2 13	6 3	...	9 43
BIRMINGHAM (NewSt.) arr	10 10	2 20	6 10	...	9 50
LONDON (Euston)	4 33		10 20		3B50

† — 1st and 3rd Class only.
s — Dining Saloon, Rugby to London.
A — Dining Saloon, London to Rugby.
B — Breakfast Saloon, Birmingham to London.
D — Dining Saloon, London to Birmingham.

THERE ARE NO SUNDAY TRAINS BETWEEN LICHFIELD AND SUTTON COLDFIELD.

Early train timetables were densely printed and often hard to decipher. This problem was exacerbated by the fact that many parts of the country ran on different times, and not the consistent Greenwich Mean Time that we take for granted today.

OVERLEAF: Historian and presenter Ruth Goodman about to depart Sheffield Park station on the Bluebell Railway in Sussex.

passenger service, but the Great Western Railway had a more fundamental problem on its hands. In the nineteenth century, throughout Britain, towns and cities set their clocks to local mean times, based upon astrological observations. This meant that noon did not occur at the same time in Exeter as it did in Bristol, and the time in Plymouth was a full twenty minutes off that in London. Local clocks reflected these differences.

This was a problem that was already requiring the attention of drivers and signalmen directing mail coaches on their regular, timetabled runs. The railway companies addressed the matter by issuing the guards with adjustable watches that could be moved forwards or backwards the requisite number of minutes as they passed through local time zones. Early editions of *Bradshaw's Railway Guide* consistently give local timings that appear to show west to east journeys taking significantly longer than east to west, as a direct result of the differences between these local time zones. Inevitably, a decision had to be taken to adopt Greenwich Mean Time all along a line, rather than reflecting the local time in the area that the line passed through. However, confusingly – and highly disruptively – this was a decision that was taken by different railway lines at different times.

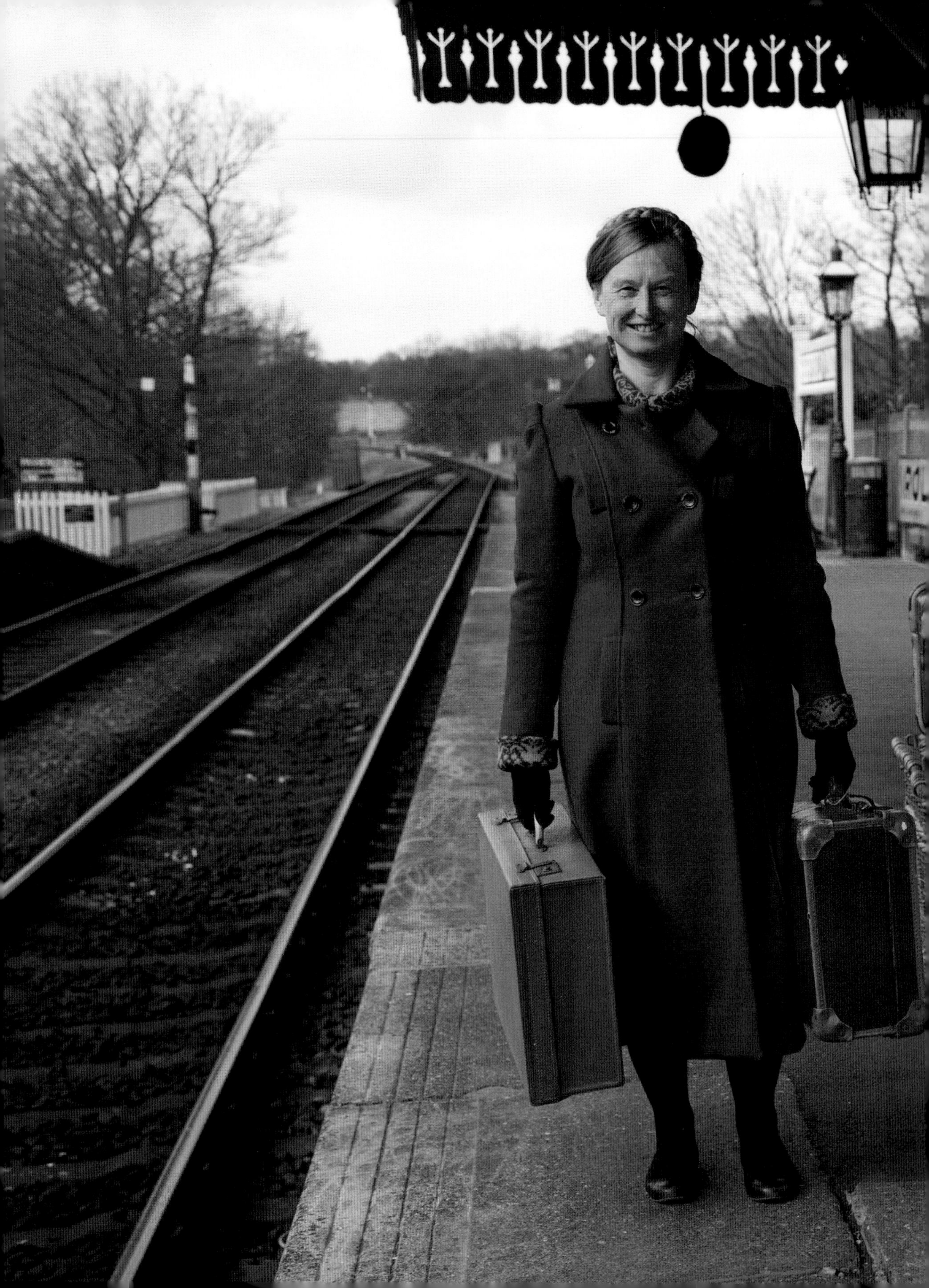

Unsurprisingly, those with the most to gain from such a chronological rationalization were the east to west lines, and these were the first to make the change to standard Greenwich Mean Time. The Great Western announced its intention to run forthwith in this way in 1840. Its timetables, also, would only give the standard time. Other lines began to follow suit, but it was an extraordinarily confusing decade for railway users, with some lines using local times and others, often connecting with or running alongside, using Greenwich Mean Time. Meanwhile, the towns and cities that the trains ran through might stick with their local time, or they too could have changed over to what was increasingly called 'railway time'. Some stations tried to ease the situation by providing clocks that showed both local and railway times, adding a second minute hand. To make a connection between two services, a passenger needed to know what time each of the two railway companies kept, the local time where he or she boarded the train, the local time of the connection, and the local time of the final destination. The clocks that they encountered during this journey might display railway time or local time or both, probably without any indication upon the clock of which was which. By 1855, fortunately such problems were rapidly easing. The various railway companies, nagged in part by the Railway Clearing House, had fallen into line and, rather more extraordinarily, so too had ninety-five per cent of Britain's towns and cities. One after another, they abandoned their own traditional times and moved over to 'railway time'. The law was not to change until 1880, but by the time it was finally introduced, to all intents and purposes the railways had already standardized time across the country. It was just one of the many shifts from a local to a national viewpoint that the railways were to bring.

Whilst information about the running of trains was based largely upon pocket watches, notebooks and timetables, information about the carriage of passengers was managed through tickets. '*Joseph purchased five little slips of paper – intrinsically worth about one farthing – for the enormous sum of nine pounds and ten shillings sterling*', wrote John George Freeman in his journal in 1873.

The concept of the ticket is a rather odd one, when you stop to think about it: a small slip of paper or card that gives you the right of access to a specific service, regardless of any other consideration. It takes no account of who you are or why you wish to use the service and it has no intrinsic value of its own. The lack of a ticket leaves you out in the cold, perhaps literally. Cash itself is useless if you cannot convert it into a ticket.

OPPOSITE: Early railway train tickets came in an abundance of colours and type-styles. There were different tickets for every class of travel and each different type of journey.

"ONE AFTER ANOTHER, THEY ABANDONED THEIR OWN TRADITIONAL TIMES AND MOVED OVER TO 'RAILWAY TIME'."

OPPOSITE: Historian and presenter Ruth Goodman purchasing old-style train tickets in the vintage booking office at Sheffield Park station.

The early railway companies were of course not the first organizations to issue tickets, but they were soon the most prolific of ticket sellers by quite some margin. Additionally, their tickets were likely to be the first examples that many people had ever encountered. Newcomers to the system were often taken aback – even offended – by being asked to produce the paper proof of their purchase. They had paid in good faith and now here was someone questioning their right to travel and even their honesty – or so it seemed.

Indeed, in the first half of the nineteenth century, even the idea of paying cash up front was not all that familiar. Most day-to-day purchases were carried out on credit. People patronized a small number of trades' people and kept an account with each that was settled periodically. This is why, for example, Mrs Beeton in her famous housekeeping manual advised keeping accurate records of all deliveries from butchers and grocers and checking them off against their later bills. Credit arrangements in the early nineteenth century were not restricted to food shopping. The wealthy, in particular, kept accounts at their tailors and dressmakers, milliners, shoemakers and jewellers, as well as at the local hostelries and stables. A stranger arriving in town of course might well be expected to pay up front in cash, but the wealthier and more well known a person was, the larger was the area in which people would provide goods and services on credit. The wealthy gentleman, the local factory owner or the member of parliament turning up at a

> "THE WEALTHIER AND MORE WELL KNOWN A PERSON WAS, THE LARGER WAS THE AREA IN WHICH PEOPLE WOULD PROVIDE SERVICES ON CREDIT."

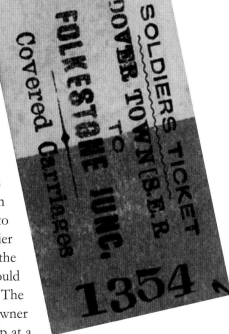

Early rail tickets could be very prescriptive and exact about whom they would carry and by what means. This example is a 'soldier's ticket', specifying conveyance in 'covered carriages'.

railway station might have been tempted to wave off other requests for payment with an airy 'put it on my account' – but the railways did not run accounts, they sold tickets…

The railways were at the forefront of new ways to do business, and selling tickets was but one example of many. Requiring payment up front and administering that payment in a bureaucratic, impersonal way was a very modern approach, and many people had to be coached through the process.

'All preliminary words are not only a waste of time, but quite unnecessary; the clerk sits at the counter for the purpose of ascertaining the place you are bound for, the class you wish to travel by, and the nature of the journey, whether single or double. The readiest way, therefore, of making yourself understood, is to apply for your ticket somewhat after this manner, 'Bath – first class – return', or whatever it may be.'

This was the advice given in the *Railway Traveller's Handy Book* of 1862. The manual also took pains to point out that *'the ticket is a voucher that the traveller has paid his fare, and its non-production at the end of the journey entails the necessity of paying a second time.'*

The first tickets were, like those of the stagecoach, handwritten receipts made out individually by the ticket clerk. Issuing the tickets was a time-consuming process. Coaches carried around a dozen passengers, but trains could transport hundreds and slow ticketing soon became a problem, with long impatient queues developing at popular stations. The handwritten system also offered unscrupulous ticket clerks an opportunity to defraud the railway companies by claiming, for example, to have sold thirty tickets when they had in fact written out thirty-five, and then pocketing the money from the additional five. The solution to the problem, and one that was to serve for 150 years, was put together by Thomas Edmondson. He was a trained cabinet-maker who managed to get one of the first station master jobs on the Newcastle and Carlisle railway, although interestingly it was the Manchester and Leeds Railway that first took up his idea. The idea was simple enough: sequentially numbered tickets – but Edmondson used existing technology to create the new system affordably and reliably. He began with a uniform size and shape of ticket, so that they could all be processed by the same machines. The size does not sound particularly standard now – one and seven thirty seconds of an inch wide by two and quarter inches long and one thirty second of an inch thick – but it worked. These are not numbers that roll off the tongue, but they fitted the commercially available pasteboard

PREVIOUS PAGES: Preserved steam locomotive 45305 heads the Cumbrian Mountain Express through Armathwaite on the Settle to Carlisle railway.

"THE FIRST TICKETS WERE, LIKE THOSE OF THE STAGE COACH, HAND WRITTEN RECEIPTS."

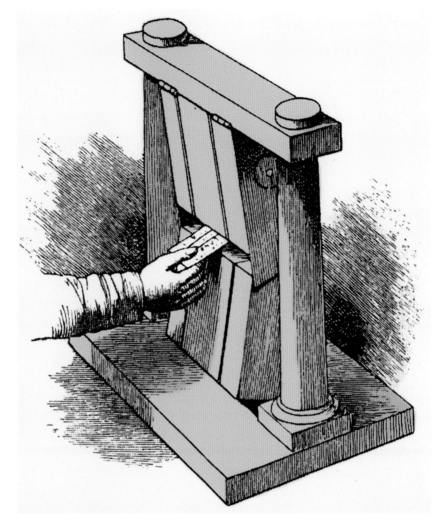

The first ever automatic railway ticket stamping machine, designed to be used in conjunction with the mass-produced, standardized tickets of Thomas Edmondson.

stock, could be printed by small manageable printing presses and yet were large enough to carry all the pertinent information. Each station required its own specially printed ticket stock of many different types. Each local destination, and the more popular distant stations, required a minimum of four differently printed tickets – child, adult, single and return. Where first, second and third class services were offered, the number of tickets needed could rise to as many as twelve pre-printed types per destination.

Each separate type of ticket to and from each pair of stations was numbered in sequence, beginning with the first ticket ever issued, reading 0001. Controlling so many different types of ticket required strict organization, but was not especially difficult. Each station, and at busy stations, each group of clerks, had a wooden ticket rack with each of the ticket types carefully labelled. The numbered tickets were loaded into the rack in order and used in strict number rotation, so that 0456 followed 0455, and so on. In addition to a serial number, each ticket had printed upon it the origin and destination, the class of travel and whether it was for an adult, a child, a single or return journey. Colour bands, typefaces and occasionally other graphic images helped people to quickly differentiate between types, and as each ticket was issued it was date-stamped with the day of travel.

Edmondson's pasteboard tickets first went into service in 1840 and only two years later became standard right across the industry, employed by all the railway companies. They survived the myriad of company mergers that gradually reduced the number of companies down to what became known as 'The Big Four' in the early twentieth century and even the nationalization of the network to become British Rail in 1948. Indeed, Edmondson's tickets were only replaced after the new APTIS ticketing system (short for Advanced Passenger Ticket Information System) was introduced in 1986, just as I began my own brief railway career. I arrived as a newly minted ticket clerk to find a shiny new machine in place, printing out thin card tickets with an orange band at both top and bottom. Meanwhile, the cupboard at the back of the office was still chockfull of unused Edmondson pasteboard ticket stock.

THE ROYAL MAIL

Internal communications aside, the railways were vital conduits of the nation's correspondence from 11 November 1830, when the first Royal Mail consignment travelled along the Liverpool and Manchester line. The Post Office valued both speed and security and the railway was able to offer both. Until that November day, the Royal Mail had been limited to the speed of a coach and horses – seven to eight miles per hour in summer when the roads were dry and around five miles per hour in the muddy winter months. The mail coaches ran along regular routes at regular times and made easy pickings for highwaymen. Security came in the form of a guard dressed in a bright red coat and a tall black hat, armed with a pair of pistols and a blunderbuss. He was also equipped with an adjustable timepiece, a notebook to record the arrival and departures, and a large brass horn that he could sound to tell toll-gate keepers to open up in plenty of time to let the mail coach through at speed. Stops en route to change horses were slick affairs that were timed to the second, while mailbags were loaded and unloaded. Mail for

The improvement in the road network in the mid-eighteenth century led to the introduction of the mail coach in 1784, providing a combined passenger and mail delivery service.

intermediate places was flung off the coach whilst on the move, with new bags snatched from the outstretched arms of the local postmaster. It was as speedy and reliable a service as good organization and resources could achieve in a horse-drawn world. Letters could move from Bristol to London in just sixteen hours at a cost of around 4d.

The introduction of the railways made an almost instant impact on the way that mail was delivered nationwide. Wherever the new lines ran, the mail coaches rolled to a halt. By 1846, the last of the coaches pulled out of London bound for Norwich. A few hung on a little longer on cross-country routes as yet unserved by suitable lines, but the echoes of the post horn were fading fast. Safely tucked into fast-moving, sturdy lockable wagons the Royal Mail could move at over double the speed. There was another benefit to railway transport, too – the possibility of processing that mail en route.

The first experiment with a travelling post office took place in 1839 between Birmingham and Warrington, upon the Grand Junction Railway.

Post office workers sorted the mail inside a converted horse wagon as they thundered along the new iron rails. This approach could cut several hours off the time it took to get a letter from sender to recipient. The traditional pattern of postal work was for the incoming letters to be gathered up in local centres and sorted by a worker into different packets, which were then dispatched in various directions. A travelling post office worked as a regional office gathering up the mail along its journey and sorting as it went, covering ground before anyone yet knew which packet it would finally end up in. By 1852, there were forty full-time clerks at work upon a number of routes criss-crossing the country. However, by then the whole nature of the post had changed as well – the stamp had been invented and the 76 million letters that were processed in 1839 had become a staggering total of more than 350 million.

The Royal Mail coach service, begun in the 1780s, flourished until the coming of the railways in 1830. This picture shows the London to Louth, Lincolnshire, coach being loaded onto the railway and the four horses which would have drawn it being taken away.

THE PENNY BLACK

In the early part of the nineteenth century, letters were carried by the Post Office for free – at least, if you were an employee of a government office, a member of parliament or one of a small number of other fee-exempt groups. These included those letters carried on that first 1830 run. Otherwise, postage rates were charged that were based upon a rather complicated scale of weights and distances. The system was not cheap, either. The postal service was viewed as a moneymaking operation by the government – one paid for not by the sender of the letter, but by its recipient. Middle and upper class letter writers tried to keep their costs down by writing in very tiny handwriting and using every tiny available space on the paper. Many letters were 'cross-written', wherein they were first written on with the paper one way up and when the page was full it was turned ninety degrees and written on again over the top. The resulting spiderlike text could be deciphered by holding the paper first one way then the other. The working classes almost never sent letters at all.

A rationalization of the postal pricing policy began in 1839. This involved the complete abolition of the free carriage of mail and introduced significantly cheaper flat rates. On 10 January 1840, the service became known as the 'Penny Post' and in May of that year the world's first stamp was issued. This was a pre-paid voucher that could be easily affixed to the letter, entitling it to carriage by the Royal Mail from anywhere to anywhere else in the country. The reform of the system was masterminded and directed through the political jungle by Sir Rowland Hill assisted by Henry Cole, who both seem to have approached the business of revolutionizing the national mail system in the context of a great social reform. Many of the old guard were horrified, claiming that even enormous growth in the volume of mail could not compensate in revenue for the new, cheaper postage rate. These doubters had a point – it did indeed take stupendous growth over as long as thirty years to return to the previous level of revenue income. However, Sir Rowland Hill was looking beyond pure commercial concerns; he had an unprecedented vision of the mail as a public service that would facilitate business and personal communications, connecting Britons everywhere for the good of all.

The idea for the postage stamp was drawn in part from a system used by the tax departments of government, in which taxed goods such as paper or newspapers were 'stamped' to prove that they had been assessed and the attendant duty paid. The 'Penny Black', as the new stamp was to be known, would carry the word 'postage' across the top to highlight that

OVERLEAF: The Foxfields train from the television series, in full steam. This preserved locomotive runs along the Foxfield Railway near Stoke-on-Trent.

PENNY BLACK, PENNY RED

The first Penny Blacks were printed in sheets without perforations and had to be cut out with scissors. They also proved rather easy to re-use fraudulently. So, just one year after its groundbreaking release, the Penny Black was replaced with the Penny Red, upon which the post office franking showed up more easily.

However, by then over sixty-eight million Penny Blacks had been printed and the British public had taken to the whole system with great enthusiasm. For the first time the Royal Mail had become truly accessible – even to the working classes – meaning that a true communications revolution had come about. As Victorian literacy levels increased rapidly, the introduction of cheap stamps, combined with an easy to understand system and speedy secure railway transport, meant that information flowed across the country as never before.

The first ever British stamp, the Penny Black, was printed in vast quantities but could be easily counterfeited.

The subsequent Penny Red offered significant advantages over its predecessor, in that it could be easily torn from a sheet and showed up postmarks without difficulties.

this was not a tax stamp. Initially, Sir Rowland Hill sought a design for the stamp by holding a competition, but the results were disappointing, as none of the potential designers seemed to grasp what was needed in order to prevent fraud whilst maintaining easy recognition.

In the end, Hill came up with something himself. His design was based upon an engraving of the young Queen Victoria, which had in its turn been taken from a portrait made of her some years earlier, when she was still a princess and just fifteen years of age. It was a distinctive profile image that needed no further explanation. Ever since then, British stamps have used a profile of the reigning monarch as their standard design. Other nations that subsequently copied the idea of a pre-paid, single flat-rate postal system have all put the name of their nation upon their stamps, but for British stamps the image of the reigning monarch is still considered to be sufficient as a means of identification.

The heyday of the Travelling Post Office (TPO) came in the years surrounding the First World War. The postal sorting vans ran on 130 separate routes both by day and night nationwide, and as war began to send sons, fathers and brothers far away from home, the mail trains became central to more people's lives than ever before. Twelve and a half million letters per week arrived from all corners of the country to a specially built sorting office at Regent's Park, London, before a shuttle of trains carried them down to the ports. The Army Postal Service brought back treasured replies from loved ones fighting abroad. Despite fears about the leaking of sensitive information and the effects of bad news upon morale back home, there was never any doubt in the government's mind that the mail had to get through. Seventy-five years on from the introduction of the Penny Black and the beginning of railway-carried mail, the population of Britain had become wedded to the idea of keeping in touch. Silence from distant friends and family was unthinkable.

Both in war and peacetime, London was the major hub of the daily postal operation. The evening's mail was gathered from all over the capital and was then despatched across the regions overnight, ready to be delivered in time for breakfast the next day. Day mail trains carried post between the more distant parts of the country, often bringing it down to London for re-sorting and speeding out again in time for an afternoon delivery. At this time, most towns and cities had two mail deliveries a day. However, central London enjoyed four, with a few favoured business-orientated areas having as many as six separate deliveries of mail a day. In the central business areas of the city, it was possible to hold entire

> "BOTH IN WAR AND PEACETIME, LONDON WAS THE MAJOR HUB OF THE DAILY POSTAL OPERATION."

conversations by post in a single day, almost rivalling the speed and convenience of modern email.

As mail was emptied out of post-boxes up and down the country, a preliminary rough sorting took place locally that separated it out into basic regions. The mail was packed into stout leather pouches, weighing anything from twenty to sixty pounds. The pouches were sent to the station, where they were joined by other pouches from other local offices and bundled together into mail sacks. The sacks were then hauled onto the relevant train and the journey began.

Postal workers gathering and sorting mail in a very early travelling post office. The work was hectic and chaotic aboard a constantly jerking train.

In terms of systems, very little changed aboard TPOs over the decades. In the image above, workers are sorting out the mail for the night postal train, London, November 1931.

Inside the TPO, wooden racks lined the walls, with a narrow waist-high bench running in front of them. The clerks mostly stood to do their work, giving them the reach required to work at speed, slipping letters into an array of a hundred or more pigeon holes in front of them. Each carriage on a dedicated mail train processed the letters for a different area, so as sacks arrived, labels were carefully examined. Some would be sent to the other end of the train while others were opened and pouches then ferried to the correct section. The work involved a lot of heavy lifting on a moving, jerking train.

Sorting clerks had to memorize all the postal districts on their routes and know which local office handled which. Incomplete addresses required prodigious local knowledge of the geography of the country and the organization of the postal system, if they were to be correctly sorted. Despite the difficulties of working on a moving train, clerks processed an average of 2,000 letters each per hour at an accuracy rate of ninety-nine per cent, while working under great pressure. It was relentless work. The lighting was frequently inadequate, the heating temperamental and catering facilities somewhat rudimentary. But TPO staff had a reputation for camaraderie. As the train thundered through the countryside, mail sacks were picked up and dropped off en route. By the early twentieth century, the sacks were generally thrown off the train without it even stopping.

The year 1886 had seen the invention of 'the apparatus'. Each TPO carriage was fitted with an extendable net next to a door. Local postmasters hung their mail bags on hooks at specified places on the trackside, and as the train approached the staff on board extended the net, whisking up the sack as they passed and dumping it inside the carriage with some force. Sorted mail being dropped off along the way was attached to an arm that extended three feet out to the side the carriage. A net on the trackside caught the sack as the train whipped past. The whole operation was heavy, fast and distinctly scary. Many postal workers preferred to keep their distance. Collin Mellish worked with the same system in the 1960s and describes the procedure as follows:

> 'The postman who was at the back of the train used to look out of the train and he'd know every sort of mark and house and tree.... and then, where the pickup point was there was a white board on the side of the track... he used to ...push the lever down on the side of the train, and this net used to come out and it'd take... maybe thirty seconds to a minute after that before it picked up the actual mail bags.'

Mellish also recorded the common practice of postal workers keeping one net outside the train for the whole journey. This was kept full of milk and kippers and was used as a sort of communal fridge. This was the world of W. H. Auden's famous poem 'The Night Mail' and the short film of the same name that it was written to be part of:

> This is the Night Mail crossing the border,
> Bringing the cheque and the postal order,
> Letters for the rich, letters for the poor,
> The shop at the corner and the girl next door.
> Pulling up Beattock, a steady climb:
> The gradient's against her, but she's on time.
> Past Cotton-grass and moorland boulder
> Shovelling white steam over her shoulder
> Snorting noisily as she passes
> Silent miles of wind-bent grasses.

The film was produced by the GPO film unit in 1936, with the poem

Mail 'on the fly': a rare illustration of the UK catcher pouch mechanism that enabled GPO mail trains to take post bags on board without stopping or even slowing down.

written by Auden to match the graphics. Benjamin Britten wrote the score, again to match the footage. Both the music and the poem, as well as the narrator Stuart Legg, all matched their tempo to the sounds of the train. If you have ever travelled on or behind a steam locomotive, you will know how uncannily accurate the whole work of art is. The first four lines sound like an engine on the flat gradually picking up the pace, then almost with a start the beat changes, 'pulling up Beattock' slow and laboured, almost panting, as suddenly the engine is working much harder to haul us up. Gradually, the speed returns and the rhythm relaxes, as the summit is reached and we are sailing steadily easily on.

The film was a celebration of the whole working life of the TPO with later verses, still set to the rhythm of a speeding train, listing the huge variety of mail, personal and business, trivial and earth-shattering, that the train carried through the night.

However, thirty years later the moment had passed. The 'apparatus' saw its last use in 1971, as the increasing speeds of trains made it too dangerous to use. However, by then the travelling post offices were also in steep decline, as road transport finally became quick and reliable enough to take advantage of its greater coverage of the country. Soon mail lorries took over route after route, just as once upon a time the railways had taken over from the road-based, horse-drawn coaches. The last TPOs limped into the twenty-first century over a hundred and seventy years after that first experiment was conducted in a converted horse-wagon on the Birmingham to Warrington railway line.

OVERLEAF: A poster produced for the London, Midland & Scottish Railway (LMS), to promote the Euston to Holyhead Irish mail trains. The poster shows a steam locomotive hauling a train by night, with the sea and a mountain seen in the background.

LMS

THE IR

8.30 a.m. EUSTON to HOLYHE
8.45 p.m. EUSTON to HOLYHE

BRYAN DE GRINEAU

SH MAILS

an de Grineau

12.15 noon HOLYHEAD to EUSTON
12.13 night HOLYHEAD to EUSTON

LONDON MIDLAND & SCOTTISH RAILWAY COMPANY

THE NEWS

Newspapers were a big part of the very first mail to be transported by train. In the early years of rail travel, every newspaper printed had to be conveyed, before sale, to a revenue office, where it was taxed and a revenue stamp applied. This 'stamp duty' entitled the newspaper to free carriage by Royal Mail as many times as people wished. Therefore, many of these early newspapers had multiple readers spread out across the country, as people sent them onto their friends – which was probably just as well, because they were quite pricey articles. In addition to the stamp duty, newspaper proprietors had to pay tax upon the paper and tax upon newspaper advertising, more than doubling cover prices. For example, in the course of 1851 *The Times* paid around £66,000 in stamp duty, £17,600 on paper duty and £24,000 on advertising duty. Printing technologies were also slow and laborious, which both added to the costs and limited

A mid-Victorian edition of *The Times* of London newspaper. Known as 'The Thunderer', this was both the longest standing and most influential British newspaper of its time.

William Henry Smith – the first and greatest of the new breed of British newspaper wholesaler. His name lives on to this day in the railway stations and high streets of Great Britain.

the size of each newspaper print run. However, despite all this, newspapers were exceedingly popular. Around fifty separate titles were published in London at this time and a further hundred were spread across the rest of the country. *The Times* was the leading London paper by quite some margin, and outside the capital the *Manchester Guardian* (later to become just the *Guardian*) was by far the most well known, even enjoying an international reputation. Circulation numbers were necessarily fairly small – even for the big players – and positively tiny for most of the other titles, which might have total readerships of less than a thousand. However, the railways, from the very first mail run, offered new opportunities for expansion. It was primarily the London papers, and especially *The Times*, that were able to make the most of fast regular railway transport to expand their customer base. They did this by extending their readerships out into the provincial towns and cities, sending parcels of newspapers out early in the morning along the rails to regional wholesale newsagents.

In 1855, the stamp duty and newspaper advertising duty were removed after a long and bitter political campaign. Newspapers could still choose to pay a reduced form of the stamp in order to secure postage rights, but equally they were free not to. The London and North Western Railway, the Midland Railway and the Northern Railway Company all introduced a newspaper parcel carriage service that year at three farthings per pound weight, in an attempt to hang on to and indeed expand their newspaper business. It was a shift that favoured the new breed of wholesale newsagent, men like W. H. Smith. All along those newspaper-carrying lines, hawkers and news stalls now graced the platforms, trying to catch a new market of people on the move with nothing much else to do but

"THE TIMES WAS THE LEADING LONDON NEWSPAPER BY QUITE SOME MARGIN."

The *Daily Mail* was one of a host of new Victorian daily papers that capitalized on the expansion of the railways by targeting a new type of readership nationwide.

stare out of the window. These newspaper wholesalers also supplied parcels of papers to the hinterland of booksellers and newsagents beyond the stations.

Once the tax was removed, competition between news titles boomed. A whole raft of new dailies appeared, many of which collapsed almost as soon as they had opened. Of these, *The Telegraph*, with its emphasis on price (1d per copy), was the biggest long-term success, becoming a realistic rival to *The Times*. In 1861 the paper duty was also repealed and newspaper prices fell even further. Huge choice and cheap prices spread the news-reading habit ever wider. Wherever the railway network went, London newspapers went too, gradually chipping away at the profitability of local titles. As sales expanded nationwide, London-based journalists finally began to expand their own horizons, travelling along the same lines in search of national rather than purely London-based stories. The spread of the railways also permitted the provincial papers to gather news directly from the capital rather than relying upon regurgitating copy from old London papers. Before the railways, a London paper would inevitably be at least a day old by the time it got to Manchester and two or three days old in Glasgow. This meant that the provincial papers, whilst hot on local topics, served up only rather tired and old news from London, by feeding off the out-of-date papers from the capital. Now for the first time national daily news became the norm nationwide, as parcels of newspapers hot off the presses sped through the night on the railways of Britain.

By the end of the nineteenth century, technical innovations in printing presses and typesetting allowed the papers to ramp up their output. Free schooling for all, with the attendant improvements in public literacy, broadened the potential market for cheap newsprint still further. Gone were the days when newspapers were the preserve of the wealthy and the educated male elite. People from all walks of life were now potential customers, and journalists, editors and newspaper proprietors alike were adjusting their styles accordingly. For example, the *Daily Mail* was just one of another raft of new titles seeking to target new sectors of the public. The owners aimed their new paper at a lower middle class readership and, in a groundbreaking shift, at female readers, including dedicated articles upon subjects that they thought 'suitable' for women.

Several magazines aimed at women had appeared previously, which generally featured romantic fiction, fashion and cookery, but this was the first time that specifically 'feminine' content had formed part of a newspaper. Crime reporting formed the backbone of another batch of titles, aimed more at a working class readership. These featured remarkably blunt and lurid language. Many of these papers remained as weeklies rather than dailies, reflecting the scarcer resources of their customers. They came to be known disparagingly as 'penny dreadfuls'. Sports news papers, and sporting sections

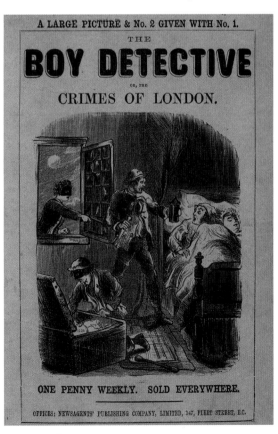

An early example of the crime-orientated 'penny dreadful' magazines that became so popular during the railway-driven proliferation of newsprint in mid-Victorian Britain.

A LARGE PICTURE & No. 2 GIVEN WITH No. 1.

THE

BOY DETECTIVE

OR, THE

CRIMES OF LONDON.

ONE PENNY WEEKLY. SOLD EVERYWHERE.

OFFICES; NEWSAGENTS' PUBLISHING COMPANY, LIMITED, 147, FLEET STREET, E.C.

"A WIDE RANGE OF JOURNALS AND MAGAZINES TRAVELLED ALONGSIDE ALL THE NEWS PAPERS."

within other titles, were undergoing a particularly rapid change. Before 1900, most of these were concerned with fox hunting, race meets, boxing matches and cricket. While both the horse racing and boxing attracted a following at the lower as well as the upper end of society, the sporting papers generally served a well-heeled audience. However, by the end of the century new mass spectator sports, football in particular, were very rapidly gaining in popularity among the less well off. As a consequence, sports papers radically shifted their coverage and tone.

As far as the railways were concerned, newsprint was an excellent freight customer. Complete, dedicated 'newspaper specials' headed nightly out of London, loaded to the gunnels and bound for all corners of the nation while catering for all literary tastes. It was not quite all one-way traffic, though: another newspaper special left Manchester packed with copies of the *Manchester Guardian* destined for Yorkshire, and along with several other provincial papers moved large consignments from their home offices into the capital. By the 1930s, it was estimated that two thirds of the entire British population read a newspaper every day.

A wide range of journals and magazines travelled alongside all the newspapers. These included political satires, women's magazines full of household hints, and even specialist publications such as *The Quiver*, which carried long articles about bible study and was aimed at devout non-conformist families. Even Charles Dickens ran his own magazine, *Household Words*, for which he wrote most of the articles himself. The cheaper production costs combined with the expanded markets offered by railway distribution fuelled a boom in all manner of cheap press. Just as the newspapers discovered that new sectors of the population were increasingly able to afford and able to read their offerings, the magazine market was discovering new potential buyers. Increasingly, 'specialist' interests could be profitably catered for, and the subject matter of the new magazines became ever more eclectic. Magazines suited railway travel almost as well as newspapers, as they provided reading material that was cheap and broken into small digestible segments that could be dipped in and out of according to the rhythm of travel. This explosion of accessible print was perhaps more visible upon station platforms than anywhere else, with titles of all descriptions massed together on open-fronted wooden stalls.

William Henry Smith had set up as a newspaper distributor in the days of mail coaches. He had almost entirely cornered the market in carrying titles out of London, when the railways arrived to offer him an alternative form of transport. In 1848, Smith negotiated an exclusive

OPPOSITE: **Presenter Peter Ginn pictured with an old grocery delivery bike in front of the W. H. Smith kiosk on the station platform at Pickering, North Yorkshire.**

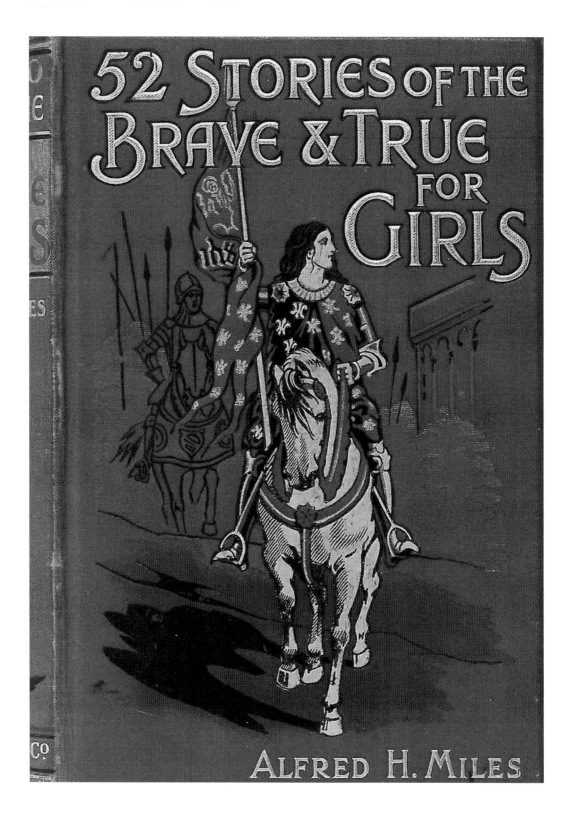

deal with the London and North Western Railway to operate all the stalls upon their stations. A host of small independent stallholders were swept away, book trade staff were drafted in and a moral purge of the merchandise took place. Out went the lurid tales of 'bloody murder' and in came respectable family titles.

> **"ALL THREE OF THESE RAILWAY PRINT SELLER ENTREPRENEURS SOON FOUND THAT BOOKS SOLD WELL ON STATION PLATFORMS."**

Other railway companies liked the look of these new W. H. Smith and Son stands, and soon Smith dominated the entire English railway station network. John Menzies was to copy the model and found an equally dominant presence in Scotland, while in Ireland W. H. Smith was eventually bought out by his general manager, Charles Eason. All three of these railway print seller entrepreneurs soon found that in addition to newspapers and magazines, books sold well on station platforms. Cheap fiction was where the main profit lay, rather than in heavy factual works – although the new print entrepreneurs continued to hold the line against 'offensive', 'indecent' or 'obscene' literature. Commercial upheaval within the publishing world had significantly dropped the price of reprints, allowing firms such as John Murray to publish his 'reading for the rail' series as 'cheap books in large readable type'. George Routledge produced a series in green covers collectively known as his 'railway library' and, seeing which way the wind was blowing, W. H. Smith went into business with Chapman and Hall to produce the 'select library of fiction', all with shiny covers and yellow backs. These innovative sellers had unlocked a whole new audience for novels, particularly as for much of the second half of the nineteenth century Smith's also offered a library service for rail travellers. By 1866, 177 separate stalls held stocks of books for loan to regular customers, and special requests could be brought in from other stalls ready to be picked up the following day. This was a particularly convenient arrangement for commuters, although many members of the public who did not use the railways joined the library scheme as well, borrowing and returning books to their local station. Novel reading, which had been the preserve of the elite, became an affordable habit enjoyed by people from almost all social classes.

THE ELECTRIC TELEGRAPH

'If only one collision of a passenger train with its sickening accompaniments of suffering, to say nothing of its heavy expenses, were prevented by free use of the telegraph, the immunity would be cheaply attained, and the cost of the improvement be amply compensated.'

So opined Mark Huish, the general manager of the London and North Western Railway, in 1854.

The electric telegraph first emerged as a commercial proposition in the early years of the railways, and indeed the railways were to be its first customer. In 1837, when the ink was still wet upon their patent, William Fothergill Cooke and Charles Wheatstone persuaded Robert Stephenson (son of George) to trial their new communication device between Euston and Camden Town, on the London to Birmingham line that he was then constructing. The incline out of Euston was initially too steep for locomotives, so this first section of the journey was to be achieved by using a heavy static engine at Camden Town and a long rope to haul the carriages along the track. A system was needed to tell the men tending the engine when to begin the pull. Cooke and Wheatstone had created a pair of devices linked by wires by which a message could be spelled out at one end by moving a needle to point to letters, and received at the other end by recording the position of the needles. The signal sent lasted only momentarily, so a clerk needed to be on hand to watch the apparatus and note the positions of the needles down in a notebook. However, despite the complexity of the system, it provided near-instant communication over considerable distances. Robert Stephenson decided in the end to stick with the older technology of pneumatic tubes and semaphore, but the Great Western railway had been watching keenly, and it was on their line between Paddington and West Drayton that the telegraph entered productive service the following year. Up to fifteen words per minute could be transmitted, but for the railways the importance of this new technology came not with the ability to transmit written words but with the potential to transmit signalling information.

We saw earlier how time was used to space trains out along the track (*see* page 170), but this system had a single major and deadly failing. If a train broke down or encountered any other difficulties on its journey along a section of track, it had no way of letting anyone behind know what had happened. At the regulation interval, a second train could be bearing down on the stranded train at speed. The solution suggested by Cooke was to use his telegraph to let people further along the line

OVERLEAF: **Railway signals on the Colne Valley and Halstead railway.**

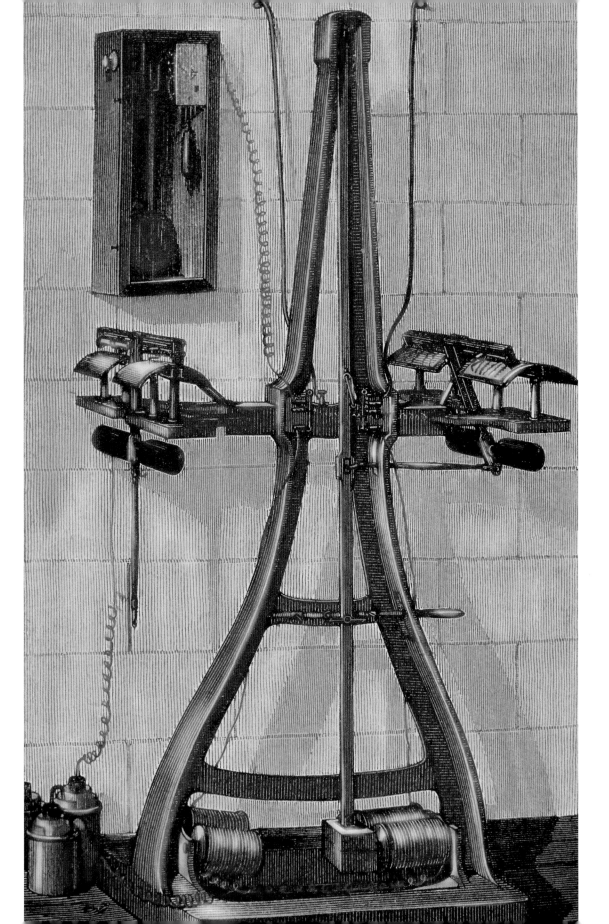

know whether a train had either entered or positively left an area. Nor did this have to be laboriously spelled out. Two simple positions for the telegraphic needle could show *'line clear'* or *'line blocked'*. As a train entered a particular section of track, it ran over a device that sent a single signal up the line, causing the needle to twitch over to *'line blocked'*. The receiving signalman wrote down the exact time and the blocked nature of the signal in his book, and when that same train left the section of track at the other end, it activated a second signal twitching the needle to *'line clear'*, which again the signalman noted down. It was thus possible to know exactly where a train actually was on the line. And the wooden signal arms set atop their line side poles could be set accordingly.

The block system, as it came to be known, proved to be a major boon to safety and, in conjunction with the mechanical semaphore signal arms, formed the basis of signalling for around a hundred years. Cooke and Wheatstone's devices were improved upon most notably by introducing a fail-safe element. In the original version of the system, the connecting wire was usually dormant, with a positive signal being sent as the train crossed the threshold. However, if a technical fault occurred, no further information would be sent, the driver would be none the wiser, and no one would know where exactly the trains had got to. By reversing the situation so that the line was positively charged when at rest and the signal was an interruption of that charge, technical faults would result in all signals turning to danger and stopping all movements – which was altogether a much safer situation. In parallel to the 'block instruments' with their twitching needles, many railway companies also installed the simple 'bell telegraph' version – generally a device that simply rang a bell at the other end of the line. The number of rings on the bell represented a code for certain information. Some of this was pure signalling safety information – such as two rings when a train entered a section, six rings for an obstruction on the line, or seven if the train was to be stopped immediately. Other codes were more for scheduling information, so that a signalman would know how to prioritize trains at different times. For example, a goods train loaded with perishable goods had a code of five rings that gave it priority over a goods train of coal wagons, which was notified by three rings. Initially, each railway had its own codes, but gradually over time a degree of standardization crept in. I was still required to memorize these codes in the mid-1980s, when I sat my own signalling exams for British Rail. One pause, two pause, four pause is a rhythm that still means to me *'is it safe to send you a passenger train?'* the first ring being a sort of introduction to call attention, the two rings asking if

SERVICE BY NIGHT

BRITISH RAILWAYS

BRITISH RAILWAY

the line is clear, and the four beats tells you what sort of train it is – in this case, a passenger train. If the track is not clear you give no answer, but if all is well then the rhythm is repeated back down the line, to show not only that the train can be sent but that you have correctly heard the request. Again, it is a system with a built-in fail-safe – silence meaning that all trains must stop.

In addition to improving safety, the telegraph provided a major efficiency saving for the railways by extending line capacity by 'an incalculable degree', according to the chief engineer of the London and North Western railway in 1851. The technology allowed the length of 'sections' to be considerably shortened. This meant that if only one train was allowed in any one section at a time, it was easy to see how more shorter sections allowed more trains to run upon the line at once. Nor was the electric telegraph a particularly difficult technology for the railways to install. Since they already owned the strip of land through which the lines ran, they simply had to erect wooden telegraph poles alongside to carry the wires. The robust simplicity of the system allowed for easy cheap maintenance and its operation required little in the way of staff training.

With signalling managed through simple codes and needle positions, the railway made little use of the telegraph's ability to transmit words. However,

A 1955 poster by David Shepherd produced for British Railways (BR) to promote the company's night services. The poster shows steam locomotives departing from a large station. Signalling equipment and signal boxes are also visible.

PREVIOUS PAGES: Presenter
Ruth Goodman having
a great time operating
the signals in the box at
Pickering station, North
Yorkshire..

their handy ownership of suitable strips of land allowed others to fully capitalize upon the invention. William Fothergill Cooke went into business with John Lewis Ricardo in 1845, setting up the Electric Telegraph

"IN ADDITION TO IMPROVING SAFETY, THE TELEGRAPH PROVIDED A MAJOR EFFICIENCY SAVING FOR THE RAILWAYS BY EXTENDING CAPACITY."

Company, and negotiated with the various railway companies for the right to build his own telegraph wire system alongside their lines. It gave him access to an increasingly comprehensive network, one that his rivals later tried to negotiate with canal companies and for which numerous private landlords would have given their eye teeth. Naturally, the ELC offices were often located either within or next door to the stations along the line. Now personal travel, letter and parcel post and telegraph communications were all centred in the same buildings, representing an information and communication hotspot in communities. Additionally, the distances that that information could speedily travel were rapidly increasing. Charles Wheatstone (Cooke's original partner and co-patentee) worked with Michael Faraday on insulating materials, and having found gutta percha to be particularly effective, suggested that coating electrical wires with the material would allow underwater cables to operate efficiently.

By 1850, the first cable was laid across the English Channel, linking Britain with France. This great breakthrough in communications was followed in 1866, when Isambard kingdom Brunel's ship the SS *Great Eastern* laid the first functional cable across the Atlantic Ocean, linking London with New York. Four years later, the first cable reached India. In 1848, it had taken around ten weeks to get a message from London to Bombay; by 1874, it took no more than four minutes.

None of the railway companies set out to bring political and cultural coherence to Britain, nor did they ever intend to facilitate the administration of the empire. However, they could probably not have imagined that they would change the nation's reading habits completely or that they would foster an appetite for long-distance chat. Yet, inadvertently or not, that is exactly what they did. The railways helped the world to become more routine, businesslike and efficient, and at the same time they introduced new forms of personal communication and connection between people of all social classes.

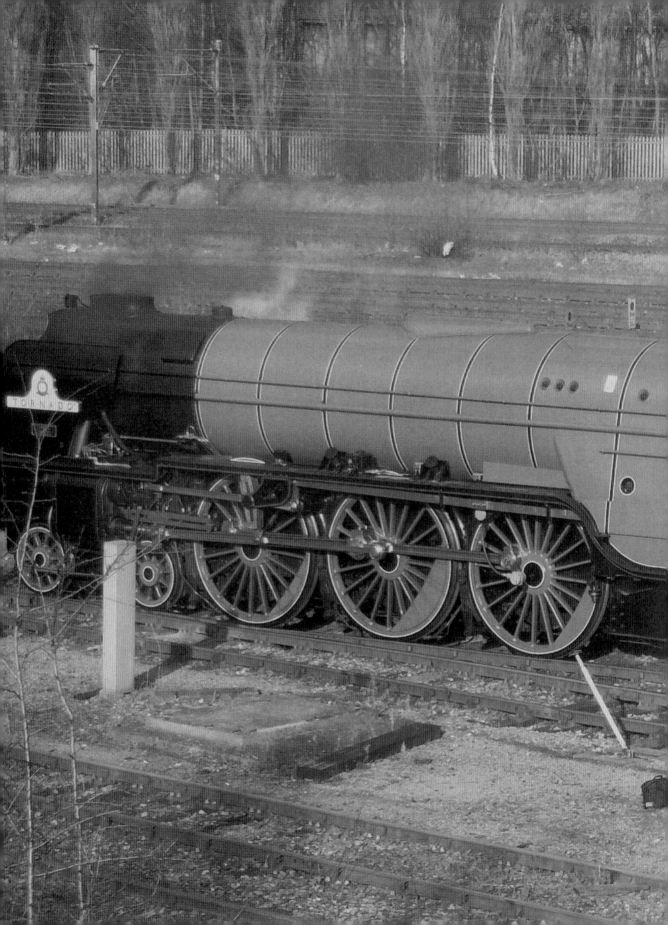

CHAPTER 5

TRADE

60163

BRITISH RAILWAYS

The railway network in Britain is a truly wonderful and remarkable achievement. The majority of the infrastructure that we use on a daily basis today was created in the nineteenth century and what exists now is only part of a much wider network that was in place during the golden age of the railways.

It is hard to imagine Britain without a rail network, but before it was built no one knew what it was going to look like. There were no committees, there was no initial policy drawn up. The railways in Britain were built by pioneers, visionaries – people who speculated that this new form of communication, of moving people and things from one place to another, would be the future. The steam railways were cutting-edge technology. They were invented and improved as they were being built and this factor had a huge impact on how they were formed.

Part of the reason why George Stephenson is cemented in railway history and is often seen as the founder of the modern railway is that he – above all others – could see their potential. Like very few other pioneers, he envisioned the railways criss-crossing Britain and connecting villages to towns to cities to ports.

At the time, there was a certain amount of opposition to rail travel – especially with regard to the anticipated speeds involved. In 1825, George Stephenson misled a parliamentary inquiry about the expected running speeds of his trains. There were fears of mental disorders being caused and air being sucked from passengers' lungs if the trains went above the 12mph limit that Stephenson allowed the inquiry to believe his running speeds would be. In reality, he expected to reach speeds of 20mph. Although people travelling on galloping horses had not had the air sucked out of their lungs, perhaps one of the real reasons for the opposition was a fear of money being sucked out of the canal network in which many people and companies had invested.

As steam-powered railways proved themselves to be viable, more and more people clamoured to invest and multiple companies were set up. Some were successful, some were not, but in a period subsequently nicknamed 'railway mania', these companies built infrastructure and laid track, often in direct geographical competition with one another. Their aim was a return on investment, and that meant attracting trade, either in the form of passengers or goods.

George Stephenson's *Rocket* **proceeding beneath a bridge during the Rainhill Trials. There was a lot of public trepidation felt about the potential speeds of early railway trains.**

"MUCH OF THE CAUSE OF RAILWAY MANIA WAS THAT BRITAIN'S RAILWAYS WERE CONSTRUCTED BEFORE THE EXISTENCE OF A FORMAL POLICY."

If a person or an item of cargo travelled from point A to point B on a single railway, there was no issue as to who received the money paid for the journey. However, if a journey incorporated more than one railway, then the division of revenue became a problem. In 1842, a number of railways collaborated with each other to form the 'railway clearing house'. Based in a building near Euston station in London, the railway clearing house was a central point where all receipts and records for journeys could be collected, collated and then the fares shared out, based on mutually agreed criteria.

Much of the cause of railway mania was that Britain's railways were constructed before the existence of a formal policy. The railway clearing house represents an early major step towards a unification and standardization of the railways. However, not all companies were involved in the project, the most notable absentees being the Great Western Railway and many railways to the south of London. The neutral ground replete with secretarial services meant that the companies that were involved could meet and discuss ideas and then informally create a roadmap for best practice.

Two elements that are well known to have been standardized by early British railways are time and track gauge. We are surrounded by clocks and, allowing for operational error, if they are all in the same global time zone, they will normally all display the same time. However, before the construction of the railways, time varied from place to place in the British Isles. In London alone there was a two-minute difference between the east and west of the city and across the country the variance was as much as fifteen minutes.

The travelling stagecoaches that predated the steam railways got round the problem by publishing the corrections needed by travellers for their timepieces en route. However, railways moved people across the country a lot faster, so the problem was literally more pressing. The Great Western Railway applied railway time in 1840 (*see* page 176), and over the next few years most railway companies willingly adopted it. However, there was a period of crossover, with many stations featuring

PREVIOUS PAGES: For many people, steam railways were all about speed. Certainly, over the decades it became one of the railway companies' great preoccupations. But attitudes were very different in the early days of steam.

Railway clocks caused a lot of confusion in the early days of the railways, with many stations and areas of the country operating on significantly variable times.

clocks with two minute hands; one to show railway time, and the other to show local time.

In 1847 the railway clearing house recommended that Greenwich Mean Time should be adopted as Railway Time, and almost all of the country operated on GMT by 1855. However, a legal case in Dorset in 1858 involving a land battle captured the public's imagination, when a man from Carlisle was late for the hearing and the judge ruled against him. The man protested that he was on time according to his station clock. Confusions such as this were ended in 1880 by the Statutes (Definition of Time) Act, and GMT was officially adopted across the whole of Britain.

PREVIOUS PAGES: Presenter Ruth Goodman in the guard's van of an old steam train. The walls are decorated with an old route map and steam pressure gauges.

'The Break of Gauge at Gloucester', June 1846. A humorous engraving showing passengers and luggage being shifted from one platform to another at Gloucester station. This was as a result of the change in the gauge of the railway tracks between Bristol and Birmingham during the so-called 'Battle of the Gauges', before tracks were standardized.

Track gauge was less of a problem than time, but in order for rolling stock to be moved safely and swiftly across the network of railways, there needed to be a single gauge. Gloucester station was a change of gauge station, where Brunel's 7 feet ¼inch broad gauge (the ¼ inch was added later) met the 4 feet 8½ inch gauge that George Stephenson favoured. Although moving passengers and their assorted items of luggage from one train to another could be chaotic, shifting bulk items such as coal and small goods like coach bolts and beehives from one gauge truck to another was simply untenable.

A commission was set up by parliament, and trials of the existing gauges were undertaken. The broad gauge, which had better stability and lower costs per ton-mile, initially won hands down. However, the narrower gauge was cheaper and quicker to build – especially in the more undulating areas of Britain – so ultimately this was adopted. This came about in large part because of George Stephenson's vision of a unified network of railways and the subsequent greater mileage of what was to become known as the standard gauge. Parliament passed the Gauge Act in 1846 and the last GWR broad gauge train ran in 1892.

"FREIGHT COMPANIES COULD USE THEIR OWN WAGONS AND THEIR OWN HORSES OR LOCOMOTIVES AND THUS HAUL GOODS ALONG A RAILWAY."

GOODS

How goods and services were to be handled by the new railways was a matter of speculation. The trackways that had been laid were seen as similar to the canal waterways that had pioneered freight transport, and so the canal companies were used as inspiration for the new iron network. Canals had charged tolls, and the very first railways – such as the Surrey Iron Railway, established in 1801 – quickly followed suit.

Freight companies could use their own wagons and their own horses or locomotives and thus haul goods along a railway. This was the initial practice on the Stockton and Darlington railway, but in 1828 the Liverpool and Manchester railway was granted permission by parliament to act as a goods carrier in their own right. Once this precedent had been set, the railways all swiftly moved towards handling freight themselves.

The railway clearing house was instrumental in facilitating the movement of goods across the network of railways, and a decade after it was established the revenue generated from goods surpassed that of passenger travel in 1852. Goods carried by the railways then remained the primary source of income for the next 100 years. However, a problem that persisted to hinder the railways was their initial formation and goods handling policy.

The railways had standard rates of carriage, which had been controlled by the government since 1840. They were also obliged by law to take anything anyone wanted them to carry as long as it could fit within the loading gauge. The loading gauge is primarily the height and width of an object (length is also taken into consideration for cornering), to ensure that it will pass safely through tunnels and under bridges. Even if an object did not fit within a loading gauge, most often the railways would find a way of transporting it.

Furthermore, unlike continental Europe, where the rolling stock carrying goods was owned and operated by the rail companies, in Britain the railways had to accept privately owned wagons – unless they were badly constructed or were in a poor state of repair. Subsequently, many of the goods wagons that were operating on Britain's railways were either owned by the companies that needed to ship the goods, such as the coalfields, or were rented from wagon hire companies. In the 1850s, the railway clearing house set technical standards for goods wagons and, along with guards vans, those wagons, although increasing in capacity, were a common sight on the railways.

To understand just how monumental the early initiatives of goods transportation were in shaping Britain's railways, it is necessary to look at how the railways handled goods in the twentieth century. The 1960s introduced the concept of what would become the 'freightliner system', which moved goods via rail in shipping containers. It was also in the 1960s, as part of Dr Beeching's generic cuts, that Merry-go-round freight trains were pioneered. These were freight trains that could load and unload on the move, hence the name, and usually carried large quantities of coal to fuel the ever-larger power stations being constructed in Great Britain. These two initiatives were to go on to effectively replace the Victorian goods practices that were still in common use. They would render obsolete the huge marshalling yards that had been built by the railways to handle the Victorian-style goods wagons.

Marshalling yards were primarily built after the Second World War and replaced multiple sites of sidings along the railway, so that the process

The last broad gauge through train leaving Paddington station, London, 20 May 1892. Although Brunel's gauge was more stable and therefore probably safer, it was considerably more expensive to install than Stephenson's narrower version.

of sorting goods wagons could take place in one location. If goods travelled on the railway in large and regular consignments – such as coal, fish or milk – the process of dealing with them was fairly straightforward. However, most goods travelling on the railway comprised of small, irregular loads, and it was these that needed thoroughly sorting.

Goods trains arriving at a marshalling yard were divided into sections known as 'cuts', which could range from a single wagon to a chain of wagons. These cuts would then be regrouped into new trains for their onward journey. Some marshalling yards were built on flat ground, but many included an incline, known as a hump, to provide gravitational power. A train entering a marshalling yard under the power of a

WHERE IS STEAM NOW?

A contemporary coal-powered power station in Japan, belching out huge quantities of both steam and smoke.

The concept of using steam as a source of power certainly dates back to the height of the Greco-Roman civilizations, if not earlier. However, the practical applications of steam did not become an industrialized reality in the nineteenth century. Steam took over the world, and changed the way we lived forever. Then, as quickly as it had arrived, it seemed to vanish. However, today our lives are still affected by steam power – not only by the legacy of the nineteenth century applications of steam such as the railways, but also by the new form of steam power that is harnessed today.

In the nineteenth century, the primary fuel that was used for generating steam was coal. Coal has a high calorific value and can produce immense amounts of heat. It can therefore release large amounts of energy. However, when coal is burnt in a fire, approximately seventy per cent of the energy goes up the chimney. The discovery of this fact led to the collection of these gases and their storage in large containers. These coal gases were known collectively in Britain as 'town gas' – which, unlike its successor natural gas, was highly poisonous.

Individual fires used for producing steam to create motion were inefficient. However, as Southern Railways and the London Underground soon discovered, centralizing the process in order to generate electricity – which could then be used to power both the trains and stations – would be a far better approach. During the twentieth century, a national grid system was created to deliver electricity across the nation. After the Second World War, as new houses were widely constructed once more, electricity took over from town gas as the favoured power source nationwide.

Much of the electricity that we use today, whether domestically or commercially, is generated by steam power. In power stations that use coal, the material is pulverized into dust in order to increase the efficiency of the burning process. The fire heats up water, which drives steam turbines, which in turn generate electricity. Although we may soon see the end of coal-powered generating stations due to the increased investment in renewables, we will not see the end of steam power.

Many large renewable solar energy stations and especially nuclear power plants all use steam power. It is also steam power that provides the propulsion of many of the world's nuclear submarines and there are proposals to incorporate this technology into commercial vessels. Although the steam being generated is produced less and less by coal, it is those early pioneers of steam technology and those innovators on the railways who refined the use of steam that we have to thank for many of the developments that enabled the industry we know today. So, next time you switch on a light, think – it may just be generated by steam power….

locomotive would be pushed to the incline. As it passed over the hump, the various cuts of wagons could be uncoupled and they would continue to roll freely down the hump and be funnelled through the points system into their respective sidings. This was known as 'hump shunting' and, as long as the goods being carried by the wagons were not fragile or abnormally sized, they could go over the hump.

The use of humps to reduce the power required from engines was introduced as early as the 1880s. Wagons coming into a Victorian shunting yard were loose-coupled, allowing for fast uncoupling and coupling with a single ratchet hand break on one side which could be fixed in the stop position by the means of a pin. When the lever was in this position, the brakes were said to be 'pinned on'. This was particularly useful, as the privately owned goods wagons often doubled as warehouse space, with goods sitting in a siding for months on end covered by a tarpaulin.

By the mid-1970s, of the 240,000 goods wagons in the national fleet passing through marshalling yards, over half still only had a hand brake to control them. Wagons going over a hump in a marshalling yard

were subjected to the laws of physics. Their weight, the wind factor and how well their axles were greased all had an effect upon their motion as they travelled down hill. As they passed through points, there were mere moments between cuts, and often the single hand brakes on the wagons were on different sides, because the various wagons had individually been turned around on turntables before reaching the hump. Marshalling yards had automatic braking systems called 'retarders' that clamped the wheels of the goods wagons. Additionally, the points could be controlled from a tower overlooking the whole yard, but the dangers associated with shunting wagons that originated in the Victorian period were still very much in evidence.

When we think of death or injury associated with the railways, our minds usually gravitate towards occasional headline-grabbing train crashes or derailments. However, death and injury was a daily occupational hazard for the workers on the early railways. The death toll in Britain peaked in the mid-1870s, with an average of 700 railway employees dying each year. By 1906, the yearly death rate for goods guards whose duties included a lot of the shunting work was 2.7 people in every thousand. Moving on into the twentieth century, approximately one hundred shunters continued to be killed each year.

In America, automatic couplings were introduced in the 1880s, when federal law dictated a need for increased safety. In Britain between 1880 and 1900, the shunting pole was introduced. Consisting of an ash handle and a metal hook, the shunting pole was designed to ensure that a person uncoupling or coupling a train did not need to go in between wagons. However, the danger of loose-coupled wagons still existed. Such a wagon is connected to an engine or another wagon by means of a chain or hook. The couple is flexible, and the distance between two wagons coupled together will vary by as much as a foot as the train moves. As a locomotive powers away and the force generated

One of the worst head-on collisions in British railway history occurred on 10 September 1874, between Norwich Thorpe and Brundall stations. Two trains were mistakenly dispatched from either end of the single line, killing 25 people and injuring 75 more. The accident prompted much criticsm of the laxity of the system which permitted such an error to occur.

OPPOSITE: October 1907: A railway shunter stands ready to couple two wagons, one of which is a Stephenson Clarke 10-tonner.

> **"A SERIOUS ACCIDENT COULD RENDER A WORKER UNFIT FOR DUTY. SOMETIMES, VICTIMS COULD FIND WORK ON OTHER PARTS OF THE RAILWAY."**

acts on each wagon in turn, an observer can see this force move throughout the train as each couple is jolted.

The use of the shunting pole facilitated an increase in 'fly shunting', which was the process of working the couplings while the train was still moving. Fly shunting was often used in conjunction with hump shunting, with cuts being uncoupled as they approached the top of the hump. One of the advantages of loose couplings was the speed at which they could be operated. Train companies introduced coupling competitions, in which shunters could compete to see who could be the fastest at uncoupling a train.

Prior to the introduction of the shunting pole, many of the deaths that occurred on the railways were due to people being caught between wagons. However, a lot of the fatal incidents – including after the poles were issued – were due to excessively long hours being worked, poor lighting and working on uneven ground. Shunting went on around the clock, and those working in the dark had a handheld lamp to illuminate their workspace. Not an easy thing to hold, while operating the pole on heavy chains at the end of a long shift during a cold, dark winter's night...

It was not until 1953 that all staff on British railways received pension rights. Death would leave a family without an income, but so too could a serious injury. Loss of limb was commonplace, so much so that the LNER had a workshop at Crewe that produced artificial limbs and the GWR employed carpenters at their works in Swindon to produce wooden prosthetics. A serious accident could render a worker unfit for duty. Sometimes, victims could find work on other parts of the railway, but often they would need to seek employment elsewhere in an era well before the introduction of corporate liability. It is a shame that there were not more jobs such as that given to the engineer Bumper Harris, who had a wooden leg. He was employed to ride the first moving staircases installed on the tube network in 1911 at Earl's Court station, in order to reassure other users of their safety.

As was the case in many other working environments that were born out of innovation and the industrial revolution, railway trade unions were formed in an attempt to battle for workers' rights. The National Union

PREVIOUS PAGES: Presenters Alex Langlands and Peter Ginn enjoying a well-earned beer in the station cafe after a hard day's shunting of engines.

The trade of steam engine driver was held in high esteem and required many years of apprenticeship. The establishment of the railway unions defined the role ever more stringently, alongside that of fireman.

of Railwaymen (NUR) was formed in 1913, when three existing unions amalgamated. It merged with the National Union of Seamen in 1990 to form the RMT (the National Union of Rail, Maritime and Transport Workers). The NUR represented drivers and firemen of locomotives, while the office workers that were involved with the railways had their own union.

However, the majority of drivers and firemen chose to remain separate, and their union ASLE&F (Associated Society of Locomotive Engineers and Firemen), which was founded in 1880, is still going strong today. ASLEF, as it is now written, can be very much viewed as a craft union representing specific workers with specific skills. The division between ASLEF and other unions can very much be seen as demonstrative of the unique role that drivers and firemen played on the railways.

Many of the drivers of mainline locomotives were older in years. This was due to the recognized and structured career path that they

took. Starting at a young age, the first job a person hoping to be an engine driver undertook was cleaning the locomotives. Engines had to be cleaned and oiled both inside and out, with ash and cinders being removed both from the ash pan under the firebox and from the smoke box at the front of the vehicle.

Boy cleaners also prepared the fires for the engines. Steam locomotives did not have keys. In order for an engine to be put into operation, it had to be heated up. For engines that were in regular service, train crews worked around the clock to ensure that the fabric of the machine did not cool down. Those that were being fired cold had to have their temperature raised gradually, as otherwise the thermal shock would begin to take its toll. It has been noted that as an A1 class locomotive is put into steam, it increases in size by as much as two inches.

Boy cleaners progressed to being junior firemen and then continued to work their way up. Firemen could gain their driver's ticket and eventually they would graduate to the controls. Drivers moved up from shunting duties and station pilot locos to branch lines and eventually main lines. The final rung on the ladder was as an inspector. This path of entry to the craft that was driving a steam engine ensured a total knowledge.

Thoroughly cleaning all parts of steam engines was a vital role that was normally undertaken by small boys as the first step to becoming a train driver. Here, a group of women volunteers clean sulphur deposits from LMS steam engines as part of the war effort.

The jobs of both driver and fireman were tough and could be hazardous. The equipment the men worked with operated under extreme pressure and accidents and explosions were common.

The very act of cleaning an engine meant that the boys setting out to become drivers knew the engines inside and out, knew what every part was, where it went and what it should look like in good working order. Drivers were not permitted to wear glasses, so the entry level cleaning jobs went to those boys who had good vision. Eyesight tends to fail later in life, and boys who had become steam train drivers but needed glasses due to eyesight deterioration remained as drivers, but were relegated to work such as shunting.

The age of steam created a love affair with many people who lived through it and many of those involved in it. Part of the reason for steam's appeal is that each steam engine is different. The crews who worked and drove the locomotives knew this and they would come to know an engine's temperament and foibles. As the years passed, improvements were made to the efficiency and performance of the machines, but sometimes it was only the engines' crews who knew how to get the best out of the loco. One piece of unofficial kit that many firemen used was known as a 'jimmy' or a 'razor' or 'spike'. Easily made by a blacksmith, it was a metal bar clamp with a safety chain that could be fitted over the blast pipe in the smoke box.

HOW DOES A STEAM ENGINE WORK?

A car has an internal combustion engine. The fuel that creates the power to make the car go is ignited inside the pistons in a series of tiny explosions. A steam engine is what is known as an external combustion engine. The fuel that gives the engine power is burnt away from where that energy is required. So, how does a steam engine work?

A steam engine will have a firebox. In here, the fuel will be burnt that creates the heat that will heat the water in the boiler to create the steam. Steam engines can burn wood, coal or oil, but in Britain coal was the main fuel used for steam locomotives. The firebox is connected to a smoke box. The smoke box acts as a baffle and stops the majority of red hot sparks and certainly larger cinders that might cause accidental fires from leaving the engine via the chimney. The smoke box also has a blower to create a draw when the engine first starts and to stop fire and smoke from entering the cab. Once the engine is underway, the blower can be stopped.

The hot gases that pass from the firebox to the smoke box do so via lots of small metal tubes. These tubes pass through the boiler and as they heat up they in turn heat the water up. The tubes have a large combined surface area heating the water. As the water reaches boiling point, it produces steam, which is collected in a dome on top of the engine. As steam technology advanced, many improvements were made. Steam is wet and there is a danger that when it touches something cold it will condense and turn back into water. To prevent this, most steam engines in the twentieth century were fitted with superheaters that heated the steam beyond boiling point and effectively dried it out.

Once the steam is produced, it travels through a steam pipe and into a valve that directs it into the pistons. The pistons are located at the front of the engine on each side and are connected to the large drive wheels by rods. The drive wheels also regulate the valves, so that when the piston reaches full extension the valve switches and directs steam to the other side of the piston and sends it the other way. The spent steam is routed through a blast pipe that goes into the firebox and is aimed up the chimney. This aids the draw of the chimney and gives a steam train its familiar chuffing sound.

In the cab of a steam engine there will be a fireman and a driver who will both know the route a steam train is taking. The fireman's job is to keep the fire burning by shovelling more coal in. Steam engines, unless they are tank engines with water tanks on the side and a coal box on the back, pull a carriage known as a tender. The tender holds both water and coal. The coal compartment usually slopes downwards, channelling the coal towards the fireman and the water tank is located underneath. The fireman will always be thinking ahead. He will be increasing the fire when he knows the train has to work harder, and vice versa.

In the cab there will be two water tubes showing the level of water in the boiler. There are two tubes so that if one becomes blocked and gives a false reading, the crew have a back up. The tubes are encased in toughened glass and are backed by regular black and white diagonal stripes. These stripes appear horizontal when viewed through the water in the tube, so they allow for the level to be easily read. During travel, the water level is kept topped up to make the engine work as efficiently as possible. The cold water from the tender is added to the boiler via an injector valve. This valve temporarily increases the pressure of the water being added to overcome the high pressure in the boiler. It does this using cones. Steam passes through a cone (large end to small) which reduces its pressure but increases its velocity. This allows the cold water to be mixed in and then the combined steam and water passes through another cone (small end to larger), which decreases its velocity but increases its pressure.

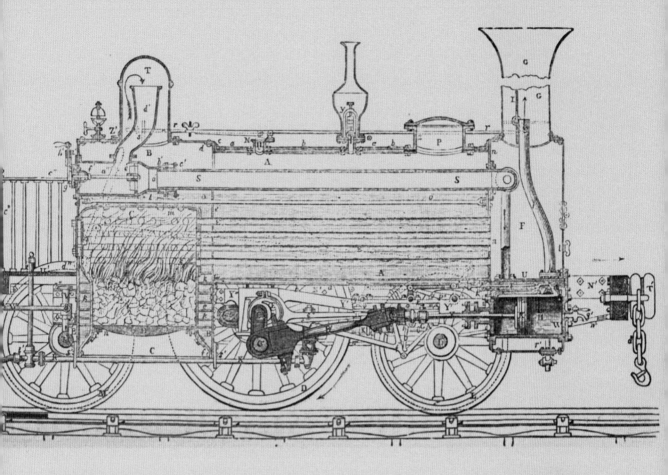

A diagram of the internal workings of an early steam locomotive engine.

With the fire burning and the water fully topped up, the driver is ready to go. He will turn the reverser screw fully on so that the train goes in the correct direction, he will let off the brakes, sound the whistle and ease open the regulator. This will channel the steam into the pistons and begin to get the train moving. Train wheels and rails are both made out of steel and there is very little friction between them. The actual surface area of an engine's wheels that touches the rails is tiny; however, their weight acting on this minute area creates enough grip to get the wheels going. Some engines have a dome, similar to their steam dome, that contains sand which can be dropped onto rails to assist traction in icy conditions.

Once the engine is underway, the reverser can be wound back. As the train gathers momentum it requires less power. The driver will know the track in the same way that a racing driver knows the twists and turns of a motorsport circuit. The driver will be able to increase or decrease the power required as the train travels along and the steam will always be there when needed because the fireman will have stoked the fire in advance.

It took many years to become a fireman or the driver of a steam engine. Everyone started at the bottom by cleaning and maintaining engines and worked their way up. Personally, having had the opportunity to drive steam engines, I say 'where's my rag, I've an engine to clean!'

The effect it had was similar to the later developments in blast pipe technology, such as the 'Kylchap' exhaust system. The bar split the blast steam from the cylinders and created a greater surface area to improve the draw on the fumes from the smoke box. Described as a 'fireman's lifesaver', it would make the fire burn white hot and improve the performance of the engine. The 'jimmy' was used by firemen working for the Great Eastern Railway on their trains known as the 'little black goods'.

First built in 1883, these simple 0-6-0 steam engines were numerous on the GER and later the LNER. 127 of them made it to British Rail service, with the last of the 'little black goods' being withdrawn from service in 1962. Their main duties were pulling freight trains, but they also saw service in France and Belgium during the First World War and were used to haul secondary passenger trains. Their longevity was due to their simple design, but they had small engine boilers, which was the reason why the firemen resorted to the 'jimmy' to help raise steam to make sure that the engines managed to run on time with heavy loads.

The lives of the firemen and drivers who moved trains of goods and passengers around the railways were not without incident. In particular, firemen faced danger in the same manner as shunters, as they often had to climb down and under the engines. However, many of the incidents that engine crews had to contend with were more dramatic than the daily shunting accidents.

A locomotive moves at considerable speed and operates by superheating steam and forcing it out of the engine under incredible pressure. If things go wrong with the steam engine, it can often be with a bang. The metal parts of the engine, especially those exposed to excessive heat, can degrade over time. If they fail, it can have a catastrophic effect. Constant inspection and regular servicing can prevent this. However,

A photograph of the Tay Bridge, Scotland, taken shortly after it imploded. The bridge collapsed on 28 December 1879, while a passenger train was crossing the bridge. All the crew and passengers were killed. At that time, the Tay Bridge was the longest bridge in the world, at just over two miles in length.

a common cause for a boiler explosion is a lack of water in the engine covering the crown plate of the firebox. Steam engines need to be constantly topped up with water, either from the tender they pull or, in the case of a tank engine, from the water tanks on their sides.

In the cab of a locomotive there are commonly two water gauges, so that if one becomes clogged and gives a false reading, the other will act as a back up. During the Second World War, 400 United States Army Transportation Corps S160 Class locomotives were deployed to handle the increased amount of freight that had to be moved on Britain's railways. The engines were designed to be constructed quickly, to run over rough war-damaged and poorly maintained track and with austerity in mind. One of their major flaws was a badly designed single water gauge that was susceptible to blockages. When the water ran low, the bolts holding the stays that reinforced the firebox crown plate failed (often a problem if a locomotive with low water levels goes over the brow of a hill). In the space of ten months, three of the engines had suffered boiler explosions.

Although drivers and firemen could take steps to prevent problems with their locomotives, failures of track, infrastructure or signalling were out of their hands. As their trains thundered along the tracks, they were reliant on the good upkeep and running of the networks by the countless individuals employed by the railways. Although most journeys were completed without incident, accidents did happen.

One of the most well-known accidents was the Tay Bridge Disaster. Officially opened for passenger services in the summer of 1878, the structure collapsed on 28 December 1879, during an extremely violent storm. The bridge had been designed by Thomas Bouch, but he had made insufficient allowances for the effects of wind and bad castings had been used in the construction of the bridge.

OVERLEAF: **Early railway semaphore signals in operation, 1844.**

"IN 1880, 15,000 MILES OF TRACK HAD BEEN CONSTRUCTED IN BRITAIN, MOST DOUBLE-ROUTE, AND BY 1900 THERE WAS SOME 23,000 MILES."

The bridge was a single-track affair, with locomotives permitted over one at a time with a speed limit of 25mph. On the evening of the disaster, a train entered the bridge after collecting a signalling token. An observer recalled watching the train cross the bridge. He saw sparks as the train entered the high girders, a flash of light – and then nothing.

The bridge had collapsed into the river Tay and had taken the train with it. It is believed that there were 75 people on board, all of whom lost their lives. The locomotive, however, was found intact underwater, within the girders of the bridge. The brakes were not on and the regulator was open, demonstrating that neither the fireman nor the driver had any inkling of the impending disaster. The engine was salvaged, repaired and then put back into operation. It gained the nickname 'the diver', and no engine driver would take it over the new Tay bridge.

In 1880, 15,000 miles of track had been constructed in Britain, most of which was double-route, and by 1900 there was some 23,000 miles. This consisted of main lines, branch lines, spur lines and sidings, all for the purpose of moving goods and passengers across the country. Small remote villages were now connected to towns and travelling to the centre of a big city and back again could easily be done in a day. The railways were changing the world.

Although railways had started out as isolated, independent entities, they had grown and begun to interlock. Engines, passenger carriages and goods wagons were all travelling along this ever sprawling system, and steps had to be taken to make sure there were no collisions. The earliest form of regulating the trains using the railways was by time. Stationmasters and signalmen, initially referred to as railway policemen, would time the trains with stopwatches as they travelled along the track. The signalmen gave hand signals, which in turn became rotating discs or boards.

This system was flawed – especially so as more trains were introduced into the mix – and an additional precaution was introduced. The track was divided up into sections known as blocks. Two trains were not permitted to occupy the same block at the same time. In the early days of the railways, signalmen had no conclusive way of knowing that a train

had cleared a block until the introduction of the electric telegraph. The telegraph system gradually came to be adopted across the railways and allowed one signalman to notify the other that a train was out of the block via a series of bells triggered by the telegraph. This system became known as the 'absolute block system'.

There had been numerous accidents on the early railways, and the process of signalling safe passage had to be addressed. However, the railways were all developing at different rates and in different ways, and it was not until a train crash in Armagh that the government took action. Known as the Armagh rail disaster, in 1889 a Sunday school excursion train was negotiating a steep climb. The driver's request for a header engine had been denied. The train did not make the climb, so the crew split the carriages, taking the front portion up the hill and leaving the rear portion braked on the track. The brakes failed. The carriages slipped down the hill and ran into another train. Eighty people were killed and 260 injured. At least a third of the casualties were children.

As the worst rail disaster in the United Kingdom of the nineteenth century and still one of the worst rail disasters this corner of Europe has ever seen, the Armagh rail disaster prompted the government to pass the Regulations of Railways Act 1889. This required railway companies by law to operate the block system of signalling (the trains in Armagh were running on timed intervals), to interlock the points and the signals so that they worked as a single unit, and to have self-applying continuous brakes on passenger trains (which means brakes on every carriage, which come on in the event of a failure). The act also monitored the working hours of employees in safety roles and required passengers to show tickets and provide their name and address upon request.

On single lines where trains travelled in either direction – such as the line crossing the Tay bridge – a token system was in operation. This system still exists today on many lines, such as the Tamar Valley line on the Devon-Cornwall border from Plymouth to Gunnislake. Tokens were physical items, often made of metal, which the driver of the train either had to have in their possession or have seen prior to moving on the track. After the 1921 Abermule train collision, the tokens took on the form of large metal keys, which when removed from the start of the line section locked a signal at the danger position. Only after the token had been replaced could the signal be changed.

Another challenge the railways had with signalling was the variety of locomotives using the lines. Trains carrying passengers, goods or a combination of both being pulled by different classes of steam engines all moved at different speeds and all had different braking distances. A signal indicating danger in the block ahead was no good if the driver of the train was unable to stop in time once he had seen it. By 1870, the semaphore signal had been widely adopted in the UK. Stop signals ('absolute' signals as they were known in the US) that had a red arm with a contrasting white stripe (or dot) and a red danger light and a green go light (the green lens was actually slightly blue, so that when it covered the yellow paraffin lamp the resulting colour was green) were installed at the appropriate places along the track. Distant signals that were similar in form to the stop signals but had a fishtail end were placed along the route to warn drivers of an impending stop signal. Should the distant signal indicate that there might be a stop signal ahead, a driver had to adjust their speed accordingly so that they could stop at the correct place.

The systems implemented on the railway, the drivers and firemen who operated the trains, the goods guards and shunters who gave life and limb reorganizing rolling stock – all these helped to facilitate trade. The world was becoming a much smaller place and, as Britain became more connected, there was major change in how goods and services were sourced geographically.

Wagons full of coal from North Staffordshire collieries, waiting to be loaded onto a steam ship at Birkenhead docks.

Goods in their raw form, such as milk and coal, were not the only commodities to benefit from the increased trade opportunities presented by the railways. Catalogues had been in existence from at least the fifteenth century, but it is a Welshman who is credited with creating the first mail order business as we know it today. Pryce Pryce-Jones was a draper from Newtown Powys. In 1861, utilizing the postal service and the newly created rail network, he took a rural business and globalized it.

Pryce-Jones sent catalogues to potential customers detailing his wares and took orders by post. He then dispatched the goods. In a world of internet shopping, this may seem a little cumbersome, but at the time it revolutionized retail trading. Prior to Pryce-Jones' business model, customers had to physically set foot in a shop. One of his most renowned products, which he patented in 1876, was the euklisia rug. A forerunner to the modern sleeping bag, it was replete with an inflatable pillow. Pryce-Jones distributed them across the world, including supplying the Russian army with 60,000 units.

The globalization of consumer products was being made possible by the steam railways that were spanning continents and the steam ships that were linking them. One domestic product that has had a major impact on the world is the Singer sewing machine. Invented in 1851, this practical domestic sewing machine was directly marketed to women as a labour-saving device. Singer offered a buy or rent purchasing agreement, which allowed reluctant customers deterred by the price or other factors to pay a monthly rental that would eventually result in ownership if the instalments were sustained.

The machines sold like hot cakes, and the way the world tailored its clothes changed dramatically. In 1867, Singer established a base of operations in the United Kingdom, due to the size of its potential market. The company chose Glasgow and set up a factory in John Street – but demand quickly outweighed supply, so other factories were soon built.

A young Victorian woman using an early Singer sewing machine.

An exterior view of the Singer sewing machine factory at Kilbowie, near Glasgow in Scotland.

Construction of Singer's third factory began in 1882 in Clydebank, Scotland, and included over two and a half miles of railway tracks. These linked the various sections of the factory and also directly connected the factory to the main line.

Although the factory closed in 1980 and was demolished eighteen years later, the Singer railway station, named for the company, is still in operation in the centre of Clydebank. The railway line the station sits upon was altered to build the erstwhile factory. In its heyday there were six terminal platforms, known as bay platforms, that allowed works trains to ferry in all the employees of the factory. These, like the factory, have since been removed, but the station is a reminder of the role that the railways played in facilitating an industry that was to alter the way Britain was clothed.

PASSENGER SERVICES

Very few railways in the world can operate exclusively as passenger services. They need the additional trade from goods in order to be profitable. However, up until 1852, Britain's steam railways' primary source of income was from trips made by passengers. The early independent train lines found it much easier to attract would-be passengers and win existing passenger business from the stagecoach companies than compete with the extensive and well-established canal network that handled much of the transportation of Britain's goods. In 1865, the year that Charles Dickens survived the Staplehurst rail crash (an event that haunted him for the rest of his life), 252 million people travelled by train. This figure does not take into account commuter journeys and represents over ten journeys a year for every single person in Britain.

The Liverpool and Manchester Railway, 1831. The first steam locomotives offered three different classes of railway travel: first-class carriages with luggage on the roofs and Royal Mail carriages at the end; a train of second-class carriages with three third-class trucks behind; a train of cattle trucks.

To this end, passengers have always been an important part of Britain's railways. They represented a major source of income to the railways, but the services provided had never been attempted before. The form and function of passenger trains was another iron in the fire of invention. The very first vehicles to be pulled by steam locomotives were very similar in style to the stagecoaches that were pulled along the road, often being built by the same companies.

Stagecoach companies also offered cheaper travel to those happy to brave the elements and sit on the outside of the vehicle. In order to compete, the railways also offered similar, cheap seats. As the horse pulling coaches on iron rails gave way to steam engines doing the work, more vehicles could be added to the train. Rather than putting benches on the outside of the first-class vehicles (although some train companies

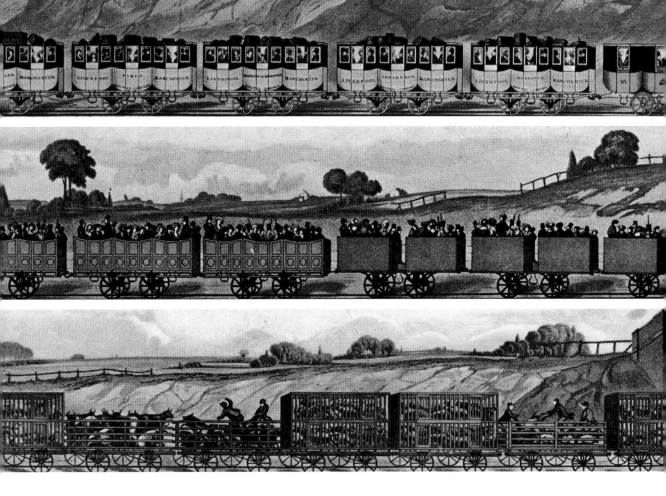

at times provided seats on top of luggage vans or seats where passengers' feet dangled over the rails), the railways created second-class wagons.

These were open wagons with benches inside and holes drilled in the floor to allow the rainwater to drain out. Occasionally a canopy might be fitted, but there were very few frills. Those who could afford it could travel in first class, those who could not or who would rather brave the elements could travel in second. Due to the sheer volume of passengers that they could transport, the railways could beat the stagecoaches that travelled by road both in price as well as speed.

There was still a large section of Britain's society that could not afford second-class rail travel. To cater to the poorest members of society, the railways created third class. Even more basic than second, the third-class passenger experience was akin to that of travelling livestock. However, the railways now facilitated huge geographical movement across the social and cultural scale. Farm labourers could set foot in cities for the first time. Trains rumbled through urban slums, showing the few how the many lived. On station platforms and in grand terminus buildings, people from all walks of life – often dressed in clothes made on a Singer sewing machine – rubbed shoulders with one another for the first time. The railways did not care about social class. To them it was all money. First-class passengers could pay more and third-class passengers could have less. It was a situation that was unsustainable. In 1844, the railway regulation act was passed. It is colloquially called the Gladstone Act, named after the future Prime Minister William Gladstone during his tenure as president of the board of trade, which was set up under the first Railway Regulation Act in 1840.

This act decreed that by law the train companies had to run what became known as 'parliamentary trains' once a day on each line that stopped at every station. The act fixed the price and the minimum speed and importantly required that seats and weather protection be provided. The act was passed on the back of one of the first significant rail crashes in Britain, which took place at Sonning in Berkshire in 1841.

The railway companies were fearful that if third class improved, their second-class passengers might downgrade their travel options. They were resistant to change, but by the 1870s there was considerable public pressure for improvement across the board. The board of trade had also made provisions for luggage allowances, the permitted minimum square footage per passenger, and minimum window sizes. Some companies, while begrudgingly providing parliamentary trains, circumvented basic improvements by creating a fourth class, but it was the Midland Railway that started the movement towards better conditions with their announcement in 1872 that third-class carriages would run with every service.

The Midland Railway was established in 1846 with an initial route from Leeds to London St Pancras. During the 1860s, the government had encouraged cooperation between the railways rather than conflict, with cases of one company's train using another company's line. It worked, but then so did competition. Following their increase in the frequency of the third-class service, the Midland Railway announced in 1875 that it would cease its second-class service. Instead, they re-designated their second-class carriages as third class and scrapped their old third-class rolling stock. They also lowered their first-class prices.

The changes were made under the company's general manager, Sir James Allport, who wanted to attract the customers away from other lines. If Midland could not beat other companies in the speed of their journeys, they could definitely beat them in the comfort of their journeys. Like the Belgian visionary Georges Nagelmackers, who wanted to provide through services across European countries via his International Sleeping Car Company (Wagons-Lit), Allport had been to

An engraved portrait of British politician William E. Gladstone by John Colin Forbes.

North America and travelled extensively on the Pullman coaches. He had Pullman, whom he convinced to visit Britain, to build a sleeping car for the Midland Railway which was disassembled, shipped over from America and reassembled in 1874.

Britain may not have had the continental space of North America and Europe, so long-distance luxury was not as much of an issue, but Allport was improving standards for all. His introduction of the Pullman sleeper car prompted a change to bogie wheels. The smaller wheels with bearings contained within their own axle box all in a bogie frame permitted shocks to be absorbed and forces to be minimized. His abolition of second class and major improvements of third class was adopted by most other rail companies, as was the introduction of the bogie wheels and gas or electric lighting.

The railways' passenger services quickly became instrumental in many people's lives. The last quarter of the nineteenth century saw population growth as well as a shift in society, with far more people working in industry and living in cities. It was a situation that led to overcrowding. One of the sweeteners that had been offered as part of the Gladstone Railway Act of 1844 was a suspension of duty on parliamentary trains. The duty was collected by the board of trade, which increasingly allowed more and more exceptions to the rule that trains had to stop at all stations.

The railway companies wanted the duty to be abolished altogether; the government wanted it to remain and be fully enforced, but they

'Travel in 1880'. An oil painting by Cuthbert Hamilton Ellis, produced in 1951 for a British Railways, London Midlands Region (BR/LMR) carriage print. The Midland railway express features a Pullman drawing room car.

also needed to fix the overcrowded city slums. In 1883, the Cheap Trains Act was passed. This relaxed the running conditions of the 1844 parliamentary trains, but required the companies to provide low-fare workers with trains to run in the morning and evening. The idea was to allow people to move out of the centre of cities and take residence in the growing housing estates that were being built along the railway lines. Some railways, such as London, Dover & Chatham, already provided worker trains, but the act ensured that they were run at the times they were needed and the fares charged suited those who would need to use them. Overseen by the board of trade, any company not adhering to the conditions set out in the act could forfeit any and all of their duty exemptions.

When the Great Western Railway introduced the all-corridor passenger train in 1891, the experience of travelling from A to B for those who could remember the early days must have seemed like a different world. A publication called the *Handy Guide* was brought out to give advice and guidance to those who needed it. The first edition was printed in 1862, and the guide was very similar to a cross between a travel guide and the late twentieth century '*For Dummies*' guides, which were brought out to aid those wishing to use the internet. The *Handy Guide* is not to be confused with the guides that were published containing all the timetable and fare information.

The *Handy Guide* instructs the reader how to prepare for a journey, what to expect, how to dress, how to deal with the toilet facilities or lack of (toilets took up space that could be given over to paying passengers), how to muse, how to sleep, how not to get taken for a ride by strangers with playing cards – in fact, it covered pretty much everything. When you consider that trains were a new entity for many – and that without corridors the compartment that one entered was akin to a cell for the remainder of the journey – I imagine that the *Handy Guide* was seen by many to be absolutely essential. However, the passengers were not alone. Railway personnel such as station masters and train guards were always on hand to look after them.

> "BY THIS **TIME, THE RAILWAYS WERE NOT IN GREAT SHAPE FINANCIALLY.** THEY WERE OWED LARGE SUMS OF MONEY FROM THE GOVERNMENT."

A portrait of Campbell Geddes (1875–1937), the first government Minister of Transport. This is a 1926 cigarette card with straight-line caricature, issued by John Player & Sons.

THE GROUPING

If the nineteenth century witnessed how the railways were born and grew, the twentieth century would see how they would live. During the nineteenth century, the railways had played a part in huge social change in the UK and across the globe. They had made the world a smaller place and consequently there was no longer room for all of the numerous railway companies that had appeared. When Britain was engaged in the First World War, the railways fell under national control. The Great War affected the whole of British society. Once the conflict was finally over, the hierarchies of Victorian and Edwardian society broke down, unable to re-establish themselves after the universal blood sacrifice. The groundwork for a new social order had been laid and changes were going to be made.

While the railways were under national control, it had become apparent that there was no need for well over 100 railway companies (by one count there were 178 railway companies), each one with its own management hierarchy and infrastructure, such as locomotive works. A man who had become a prominent figure during the Great War as someone who could find solutions to problems and get things done – such as accelerating small arms production or filling shells with explosives – was Eric Campbell Geddes. In 1919, he was appointed as Britain's first Minister of Transport to look after the roads, canals, docks and, perhaps most importantly, the railways. He was overseeing the handing back of control from the state to the companies.

By this time, the railways were not in great shape financially. They were owed large sums of money from the government for the operating costs incurred during the war, which the government was both slow and reluctant to pay. Furthermore, following a national strike by railway staff in 1919, hours and pay were altered in favour of the workers, leading to greater overheads for the companies. Many companies struggled to survive in the years directly following the war.

There was an argument for the nationalization of the railways that echoed the sentiments of a young William Gladstone in the 1830s. However, Geddes was against this seminal move, as he believed it would lead to bad management. Instead he wrote a White Paper proposing the amalgamation of many of the existing companies. The idea of amalgamation had first been proposed in the 1850s, but had never come to fruition.

The railways moved out of government control on 15 August 1921 and four days later the Railways Act was passed. It is known as 'The

RAILWAYS AND WAR

In my parents' house there is a small painting of a makeshift building in Surrey. It was to here that my great-grandfather was relocated along with his colleagues during the Second World War, when he was working in the offices of Southern Railways at Waterloo station. Having served in the Great War, he was enlisted in the home guard and their unit was tasked with the protection of a railway tunnel.

The wars had such a major impact on the railways, ultimately pathing the way to their nationalization and partial demise. However, as the saying goes, 'you reap what you sow'. Between 1850 and 1945, railways played a significant part in all major conflicts, helping to alter the theatre of war. Railways were good for moving heavy objects and lots of people over large distances very quickly. The best of the navvies who built the railways could shift 20 tons of soil each in a day. During the creation of what is called the 'permanent way', temporary track was laid to help with construction. All these factors point to one conclusion; railways can be created quickly to escalate the scale of a conflict.

The first war to witness a major impact from the railways was the American civil war. The railways had been a part of the Crimean war (1854–56) and the Italian war of liberation (1859), but in those cases they were simply used to move supplies and casualties. The American civil war (1861–65) saw the first battle won by the use of the railways to move troops. This was the battle of Bull Run (1862), which resulted in a confederate victory. Military historians have argued that had the battle gone the other way, the American civil war may have been altogether a much shorter affair.

The three wars waged by Prussia between 1865 and 1870 and the Boxer Rising in China in 1900 all saw use of railways, but the zenith of railways being used in the theatre of conflict was during the First World War (1914–18). In 1916, Britain and her allies were on the verge of losing the 'war to end all wars'. Horses and trucks were not sufficient to supply troops at the front. Something had to be done, and it came in the form of the British Light Railway. Thought to have been influenced by the Ffestiniog railway in Wales, a network of narrow gauge railway was created to aid the trenches and allow the allied powers to adapt to changes in the battlefield.

At its peak, the British Light Railway moved 210,000 tons of goods a week. There were 1,224 British locomotives sent to France and Italy for war service, and as many as 687 locomotives in total operated on the British Light Railway. These engines were either British- or American-made and, although most of them were steam driven, many were petrol powered. Indeed, even model T Ford cars were converted for use on the railways during the war.

The railways were not just confined to the western front. 625 miles of standard gauge and 128 miles of narrow gauge railway was built in the middle eastern war zone. When war ended on 11 November 1818, the British, Indian and American railways had supplied and laid 4,000 miles of standard gauge track, 878 miles of metre gauge track and 4,346 miles of narrow gauge track. In total, around 2,000 locomotives and 80,000 carriages had been used across all the gauges.

The Second World War also utilized railways, but they were not as crucial to troop movements and supplies as they had been in the Great War. The conflict, certainly in Europe, was far more mobile, with improved movement by road vehicles and advancements in aircrafts. However, the railways remained very important. During bombing raids in Britain, locomotives were not specifically sought out as targets and relatively few were destroyed. The main targets were the actual lines of communication. To destroy a railway line meant a disruption in the flow of munitions, troops and supplies. It was also the railways that helped shift 750,000 tons of rubble generated by the blitz in a five-month period, to be used as hardcore for runways and aircraft hangars.

Grouping' and it commenced in January 1923. Geddes had proposed that five or six companies be formed, but after careful deliberation the existing rail companies were grouped into 'the Big Four of the New Railway Era', as the *Railway Magazine* put it in their February issue.

The Big Four were Great Western Railway (the only company to retain a name that had previously been in existence), London, Midland and Scottish Railway, London and North Eastern Railway, and Southern Railway. They included most of the companies and troubles ensued during the bedding in period. Rivals had to work side by side, routes had to be prioritized, managers found themselves sidelined, often answering to their competitors, and engineering traditions had to be agreed. It took time, but afterwards the big four became icons during the pinnacle age of steam railways.

Not all companies were included in the grouping. Electric railways such as the London Underground and its associated lines, joint railways and many small gauge or light railways were left out, but the majority of track miles were now under the control of four companies. Geddes, whose austerity policy to regulate national expenditure had failed, resigned from politics in 1922. One proposal he had made in his paper, which had gained support from the Labour Party, was the greater involvement of workers at a boardroom level. This was not included in the final act, but unprecedented provisions were made for collective negotiations and bargaining between the companies and the trade unions.

Of the Big Four, only Southern Railway received the majority of its revenue from passengers. It embarked upon a scheme of electrification via a third rail, which made sense due to the many densely populated areas that the railway travelled through. It also meant that trains carrying commuters did not have to be fired up each day and kept warm each night. Perhaps because the railway was so reliant on passengers – mainly commuters, but often holiday makers or those wishing to travel abroad via ship – it was the first railway company to have an in-house PR department. Southern Railway's reliance on passengers, its savvy use of public relations, its advertising campaigns such as 'Live in Kent and be Content' and its policy of electrification, meant that when Britain sank into the Great Depression in 1929, Southern Railway fared especially well in comparison to the other three companies.

GWR, LNER, and LMS all relied heavily on their goods trade – especially the transportation of coal. The Great Depression primarily affected industry, and these three companies suffered the effects. Rather than dwell on the negatives, or indeed allow the public a glimpse

behind the curtain at the 'warts and all' economic situation, the railway companies chose to focus on select services and promote them as their public face. The Big Four competed with each other (often not directly), trying to offer greater modernity, speed and comfort. All the railways were aware of the threats posed by the increased traffic on the roads. Ultimately it meant that the whole situation generated an era of truly iconic steam trains.

One of the most famous locomotives of all is the *Mallard*. Its place in history will forever be assured. This is because it holds the record for the fastest speed set by a steam locomotive, clocking in at 125.8mph. The *Mallard* was an A4 class Pacific designed by Sir Nigel Gresley (who turned his moat over to a breeding ground for wild ducks). The A4s are instantly recognizable, due to their art-deco-esque streamlining, and Gresley built them for speed. The thirty-five A4s that were built were for use on LNER's east coast mainline, which linked Edinburgh and London. The LNER ran a non-stop train service on this route, which was known as the Flying Scotsman.

The Flying Scotsman service competed with the LMS' non-stop Royal Scot service, which ran on the west coast mainline between London Euston and Glasgow Central. Each company tried to beat the other in

The *Mallard* 4-6-2 steam locomotive, no. 4468. On Sunday, 3 July 1938, the locomotive reached a speed of 126 mph on a straight stretch of track between Grantham and Peterborough, achieving a new world record for steam locomotives which remains unbroken to this day.

THE FLYING SCOTSMAN

Flying Scotsman was built in 1923 as an A1 class locomotive and was named for the east coast passenger service that she was intended to pull. Over the years, *Flying Scotsman* was improved and in time became an A3 class. To distinguish between the locomotive and the service, the engine is called *Flying Scotsman* and the service is called The Flying Scotsman.

When the death knell was sounded for steam in 1955, with a complete ban on all steam on the mainline coming into force in 1968, the iconic locomotives faced the scrap yard. Although there had been some steam preservation in operation, this was the catalyst for the steam preservation movement we know today. *Flying Scotsman*'s date with the scrapyard was announced in 1962.

Recently voted the world's most famous locomotive, *Flying Scotsman*'s fame has been accumulated over the years. Although it gained much popularity during operation – especially after a number of film appearances – many of the events it undertook during preservation have helped elevate *Flying Scotsman* to a unique level in the national consciousness. As part of the acquisition deal that Alan Pegler negotiated when he bought the locomotive from British Railways, it became the only engine that was exempt from the mainline steam ban.

Flying Scotsman has had an interesting retirement. She has toured America, promoting British industry, been mothballed in an army base, been through the Panama Canal and crossed Australia. In 2004, she was acquired by the National Railway Museum based in York and has been given a complete overhaul. We were lucky enough to see how the team gets her into steam.

These engines always had a fire of some description burning in them while they were working and only ever got cold when they were due a trip to the steam works for an overhaul. However, preserved engines do not work every day. As Alex and I climbed into the firebox to check the lead plugs and the metal around the stay bolts, it had been three days since *Flying Scotsman* had last been in steam. The fabric was still warm to the touch and I was surprised at how large the firebox was, with enough room for us to stand up.

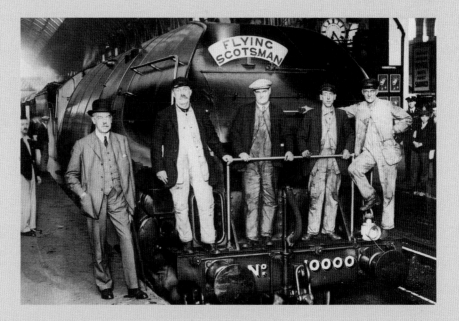

Sir Nigel Gresley with railwaymen beside locomotive No 10,000, in 1930, one of the locomotives used on the legendary Flying Scotsman service.

terms of timetabled speed, a rivalry that had started before the grouping as the 'Race to the North'. Speed has always been an important factor with the railways, ever since Stephenson misled parliament in 1825.

When the LNER introduced their Flying Scotsman service in 1928, they initially pulled it with class A1 locomotives, the first of which was called *Great Northern* and the most well known is *Flying Scotsman*. The A1s were equipped with corridor tenders that allowed the crew of driver and fireman to be swapped mid-run and facilitated the non-stop service. In time, the A1s were rebuilt mostly to A3 specifications, with a higher-pressure boiler and increased superheating surface.

These two classes, also designed by Gresley, represented the design path of the A4s. Gresley believed in horses for courses, and when he designed and built locomotives he had their role and their routes in mind. It has been said that some people could tell their geographical location on the railways based on the smell of the coal being used. Coals from different areas of the country (and the world) have different properties. Some burn better than others, some are fierce, some are steady. Welsh coal is very good for steam and had a significant impact on the Great Western Railway's locomotive performance. Softer coals produce large amounts of soot and smoke. The more impurities that go up the chimney mean the less energy that is being released from the mineral. Nigel Gresley and his assistant Oliver Bulleid built the A4s to efficiently consume coal from the Kent coalfield, which was some of the softest in use. This meant that when they ran on other coals, such as those typically used in speed tests, the A4s were geared up to extract as much calorific value from the coal as possible.

The *Mallard* set the speed record on 3 July 1938, with 61-year-old Joseph Duddington at the controls alongside his fireman, Thomas Bray. The line was limited to 90mph and the train had to slow for a junction at Essendine. Those involved in the successful record attempt believed that the A4 locomotives could achieve a higher speed and Gresley planned to try again. However, the scheduled attempt was called off when Britain went to war for a second time in many people's lives.

The Second World War again brought the rail companies together to work as a single entity. After the war ended, Clement Attlee's government nationalized the railways, along with road freight and canals, under the British Transport Commission. The commission appointed executives for each of the sectors and the one responsible for the trains traded as British Railways. Much of the rail infrastructure was damaged during bombing raids in the war, but it was nowhere near as bad as the

Historian Ruth Goodman outside Fortune's kipper shop in Whitby, North Yorkshire. As the British railway network improved and speeded up, commodities such as fresh fish could be transported around the entire country with ever greater ease.

Dr Richard Beeching, later Lord Beeching, showing off his infamous report on *The Reshaping of the Railways*, designed to make British railways profitable. Beeching was Chairman of the British Railways Board from 1963 to 1965.

OVERLEAF: Presenter Peter Ginn, standing in front of a mountain of whisky barrels at a distillery in the Strathspey region of the Scottish Highlands.

destruction of the other railways in western Europe. This served as a disadvantage, because the railways of continental Europe could more or less be built from scratch, but the railways of Britain had to be repaired.

The Great War, the Great Depression, the Second World War and the continuing austerity measures that Britain lived under until the mid-1950s all meant that the railways suffered. The British transport commission was in serious financial trouble due to the railways, which had a huge and growing financial deficit. Consequently, the decision was made to abolish it and separate out the various entities. In 1963, the railways collectively became the British Railways Board, which from 1965 was known as British Rail.

The last chairman of the British transport commission from 1961–1963 and the first chairman of the British Railways Board from 1963–1965 was the infamous Dr Beeching. Working for ICI,

> **"THE GREAT WAR, THE GREAT DEPRESSION, THE SECOND WORLD WAR AND CONTINUING AUSTERITY MEASURES ALL MEANT THAT THE RAILWAYS SUFFERED."**

he took a five-year leave of absence in order to take up his position with the British Railways Board. His job was simple; quickly sort out the huge problems that the railways were having and make them profitable. He did this via two reports. The first was called *The Reshaping of British Railways* and the second was called *The Development of the Major Railway Trunk Routes*.

Beeching's reports were based upon his studies of the operations of Britain's railways.

ROAD VERSUS RAIL

It is a common misconception that the motor car sounded the death knell of the steam train or indeed destroyed the railways. Our rail network is still one of the most extensive and well used to be found anywhere in the world – and almost all of that infrastructure was put in place in some form or another in the nineteenth century.

It is true that steam became outdated. As a source of motive power it was inefficient and had to go – and in the final analysis its demise was brutal and absolute. In hindsight, a more gradual phasing out of steam and a slower introduction of diesel-powered engines would have been more appropriate. It was not the car that replaced steam railways, but rather the internal combustion engine.

The car certainly had an impact on the railways, in a similar way that the railways affected the canals and the stagecoach companies many decades earlier. However, many of the freight companies that took goods by road were owned, at least in part, by the railways. It is fair to say that the railways adopted roads as a means of transporting freight early in their history. The charters the railways were bound by meant that transporting a huge variety of items across a network operated by a number of companies was made easier if some of the journeys between stations were completed by road. This meant that the railways employed a large number of horses and carts – and later on, trucks – to help move goods.

The first real challenge to the railways by road came just after the First World War. The railways had been nationalized and operated under austerity measures during the war. The Great Depression and the Second World War were about to follow, accompanied by a continuation of austerity well into the 1950s. Immediately after the First World War, there was a surplus of trucks in Britain, along with a more established infrastructure for refuelling and general motoring. This prevailing situation led to the railways having to compete with lots of 'man and van' companies that had no real overheads to speak of. Additionally, as the railways had to publish their charges for freight, it was easy to undercut them on price.

During the twentieth century, numerous roads were built and improved, cars and trucks became more readily available, and a nationwide network of fuel stations was created. The car took off, and steam essentially came to an end. However, in actual fact the railways are still doing well, with many proposals on the table for the reinstatement of some of the closed branch lines. Of course, cars are very convenient, but when it comes to travel across Britain – especially when travelling between the centres of two cities – nothing beats the railways.

Ever since the invention of the motor car in the late nineteenth century, there has been something of a rivalry between the roads and the railways. Sometimes, as here, time trials would be organized, in which the two forms of transport would compete against one another.

Many branch and spur lines ran regular services but carried very little passenger traffic. Beeching also fundamentally believed that there was too much duplication of routes on the railways, which may well have been a hang up from all the competing railway companies building lines in the same territory when the railways were first created. Ultimately, something had to be done. The cuts that Beeching proposed affected many of the small communities which one hundred years previously had been put on the map by the railways. The doctor was mindful that one in nine families now owned a car and road travel would only become more prolific. If both his reports had been fully accepted by the government, then Britain's railways would now be a complete shadow of their former selves.

Thankfully, the cuts were not as drastic as they could have been. Some lines managed to reopen, and those routes – such as what is now known as the heart of Wales line, which passed through a number of marginal constituencies or carried profitable freight – were spared. Dr Richard Beeching is often seen as the villain in the whole process, but he had a job to do. Many of the problems faced by British Rail, the building of huge marshalling yards to handle declining freight (Beeching recommended a system which would become 'Freightliner'), and the decision to completely phase out steam came from the 1955 modernization plan.

The plan was not a success and paved the way for drastic action by Beeching. It did, however, successfully end steam while it was still a reliable and efficient form of locomotive power. The last mainline passenger train to be pulled by steam on British railways was the Fifteen Guinea Special on 11 August 1968. The following day there was a ban on steam on Britain's standard gauge railways.

The railways were forged from visions and ambition. They were born out of competition and ultimately had to make money. They changed the world and the world changed them. Perhaps if there had been a grouping or a nationalization of the railways at a much earlier date, then competition from the roads and the air and the duplication of routes and services may not have been such an issue. However, it was those pioneering companies going head to head that gave us the rail network we have today. The railways may have lost out on trade in the twentieth century, but it was the railways that made it possible for many companies to extensively trade in the first place. At the start of the nineteenth century no one knew what the railways were going to look like; however, 200 years later I think they actually look pretty damn good.

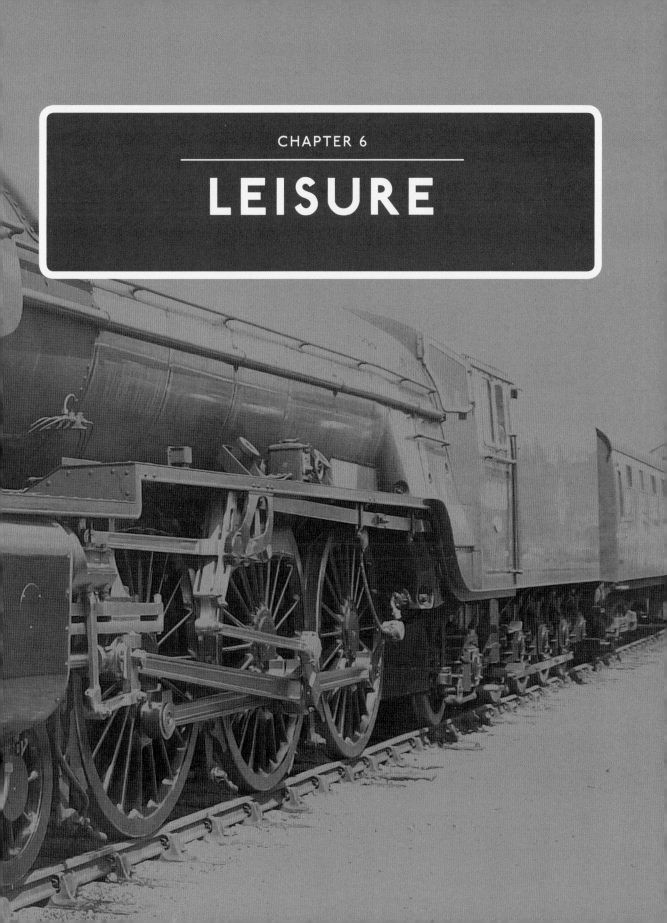

CHAPTER 6

LEISURE

Although travel on roads and canals was already well established, from the 1830s onwards railways in Britain revolutionized the movement of people and freight. They also changed the ways that people spent their leisure time. From day trips to holidays, the railways enabled mass transport over much greater distances than had been previously travelled and at greater speed, too.

Suddenly, ordinary people could access all parts of the country and subsequently the world, if they desired. The introduction of the railways brought an impact on people's lives that was akin to the mass production of the motor car and the evolution of the budget airline.

The word holiday is derived from the term 'Holy Day', and comes from the demarcation of certain days within the christian calendar as feast days. These days would have been documented in the *Book of Hours*, which detailed the division of the days and the year according to a monastical lifestyle. The book was available to lay people as well, so holy days would have affected the whole community.

The word vacation, derived from the Latin 'to leave', gained much of its meaning for a break from work during the Middle Ages. The Inns of Court in London have a yearly calendar that is divided into terms and vacations. To this day, lawyers still process from the temple over to Westminster Abbey to attend the yearly ceremony that signifies the commencement of the first term. When the lawyers are not in residence, they are said to be 'on vacation'. This vernacular of the law courts was carried over to universities.

However, the more modern perception of a holiday or a vacation, certainly as far as the masses were concerned, was forged in the age of steam. The idea of 'leisure time' very much originated in the nineteenth century. With the exception of religious pilgrimages, which were accessible to many people across society, 'holidays' had long been the preserve of the rich alone.

Having said that, the concept of 'tourism' seems to have been around almost as long as mankind has been civilized. Early forms of travel that might be considered tourism often focused on health. There is a belief that, during the Bronze Age, the site of Stonehenge in Wiltshire attracted people from across Europe in search of cures for a variety of ailments. Similarly, the Romans established many baths used for ritualistic cleansing

Health spas, such as the Roman baths at Bath, England, pictured here, were some of the earliest holiday resorts. The railways made them more accessible to a wider variety of people than ever before.

A late nineteenth century view of a typical early nineteenth century scene: a young man and woman study a map of Italy in Emil Brack's painting, 'Planning the Grand Tour'.

at the sites of both inland and coastal mineral springs. Those who were sufficiently wealthy could travel to these locations and, over time, many of these spas – such as Baiae in southern Italy – essentially became holiday destinations.

> **"THE GRAND TOUR WAS GENERALLY CONDUCTED IN WESTERN EUROPE, ALTHOUGH SOME INTREPID TRAVELLERS VENTURED FURTHER AFIELD."**

Although Roman baths had been created in ancient Britain, it was in the 1600s that the tradition of medicinal bathing was revived. Thomas Guidott established a medical practice in Bath, Somerset, in 1668, publishing papers discussing the healing properties of the water. Many spa towns were established across Britain as people increasingly began to travel and visit. There is even a town named 'Spa' in Belgium, which offers the bountiful iron-rich waters after which spa towns are named.

In the mid-seventeenth century, the Grand Tour also became very popular. The idea behind this novel holiday concept was that wealthy young men of social standing should embark upon an extended continental journey lasting for months, if not years. The Grand Tour was generally conducted in western Europe, although some intrepid travellers ventured further afield. The aim of the tour was to experience the roots of civilization; to gain an education while honing language skills and making social connections; and to collect unique pieces of art and furniture with which to feather a nest and further a reputation in society back home. The Grand Tour became a rite of passage and perhaps even a little formulaic, rather like a modern university 'gap' year. It is embossed upon the national consciousness and became something to aspire to for many rich young men over many decades.

With the advent of steam power, the world became a smaller place. Travel became cheaper and easier and there was a host of willing participants all wanting to experience grand tours of their own. Trade routes and military duties had seen people across the social spectrum travel to quite exotic locations, but not for the purposes of leisure. Now all that was about to change forever.

Meanwhile, in the worlds of agriculture and industry, steam was making just as much of a mark. Steam saves labour, in as much as it can do the work of many men. Steam engines deployed in agriculture meant that fewer people were needed to work on farms, so increasingly rural

OVERLEAF: Presenter Ruth Goodman with Glenn Fitzpatrick at the seaside.

workers travelled to the cities to find work instead. Much of that work was to be found in factories powered by steam. The agricultural year is continuous and hard work but there is an ebb and flow to the work. Sunlight governs working hours and the seasons dictate the pace of labour. Contrarily, industrial steam power is relentless and continuous. So long as someone is feeding an engine coal and water, it never stops. The immense shift from rural to industrial ways of working that steam power caused changed the pace of people's lives. In turn, this meant that relatively well-paid factory workers – especially in the industrial north – would come to feel that they needed a break. It is generally accepted that the United Kingdom was the first European country to actively promote leisure time to an increasingly industrial population. This was a population that both needed a break and had an income that could be spent on railway transport.

EVENTS

The railways enabled a greater number of people to take part in a wide range of events, from music concerts to sporting spectacles. They represented a good way of moving a large number of people a long distance in a short space of time, meaning that a big audience for a single event could easily be assembled and dispersed within a single day. Perhaps the most famous event of the Victorian period was the Great Exhibition, which was held in Hyde Park in 1851.

Following two decades of political unrest in Europe, the Great Exhibition was a display of 'the works of industry of all nations', although primarily it promoted Britain as an industrial world leader. The project was conceived and approved a mere nine months prior to its opening. The majority of the exhibition was housed in the great Crystal Palace, a giant greenhouse structure of glass ceilings and walls. The nature of the structure negated the need for lighting and meant that fully grown trees could be cultivated within the building. This impressive feature was intended to demonstrate Victorian man's conquering of nature.

The exhibition ran from 1 May until 11 October, when the structure was dismantled and relocated to Sydenham in South London (an area that was subsequently renamed Crystal Palace). During those five short months the Crystal Palace welcomed some six million visitors – a number equivalent to a third of the population of Britain. Tickets were sold to anyone who could pay. The most popular was that costing one shilling (equivalent to five pounds in today's money), eagerly purchased in volume by the emerging industrial classes. The revenue that was generated above

the cost of the exhibition was used to create the Victoria and Albert Museum, the Science Museum and the Natural History Museum at a site to the south of Hyde Park. Some of the money was also used to fund further industrial research.

The exhibition itself included diamonds, minerals, machines, utensils, farm equipment, guns, locks, textiles – pretty much everything under the sun. To accommodate the visitors, the first public flushing toilets were designed and installed by George Jennings. They cost a penny to use, giving rise to the phrase 'spend a penny', and Jennings convinced the organizers and park authorities to allow him to leave the toilets in situ after the exhibition closed. It was a wise commercial decision: the toilets went on to generate £1,000 a year in revenue.

When the Crystal Palace was moved to south London and reopened in 1854, it was enlarged and reconfigured. The cost of the move, together with the alterations, saddled the company with a financial burden it never repaid. The chosen permanent location at Penge Common was in part lobbied by representatives of the London, Brighton and South Coast railway. Due to the popularity of the Great Exhibition, the railways would be well aware of the revenue that they could earn from visitors

PREVIOUS PAGE: **Queen Victoria and Prince Albert inaugurating the great 1851 exhibition at Crystal Palace, Sydenham, London.**

After the huge success of the paying toilets at the Great Exhibition of 1851, the Victorians went on to build grandiose public conveniences at every major venue.

The unlikely looking figure of Colonel George Gouraud, a veteran of the American civil war and agent of Thomas Edison, who famously recorded a concert of Handel's music at the Crystal Palace in 1859.

to the new site. Two railway stations were opened to serve the new location; Crystal Palace High Level and Crystal Palace Low Level. The new permanent exhibition space was intended to be a People's Palace.

The new exhibition housed a host of both permanent and temporary exhibits and offered space for musical concerts and circuses. People from all walks of life could now enjoy what had once only been available to those with money. In 1859, to mark the centenary of the death of the composer George Handel, a commemorative performance of a selection of his music was staged at the Crystal Palace. These Handel festivals became a regular event, being staged every three years until they finally fell out of fashion in 1926.

The performances were colossal and only made possible by the existence of the railways. Audiences regularly exceeded 80,000, with 87,784 people attending in 1883. The first orchestra consisted of 460 players accompanied by a 2,700 strong chorus – but later choruses featured as many as 4,000 performers. The participation of the railways was openly acknowledged – even celebrated – as part of the spectacle, with a mention in the 1862 programme. It was estimated by the *Musical Times* that for the first concert in 1859, 12,000 people an hour arrived by train. That is 1,000 people every five minutes.

A recording of a Handel festival was made at the Crystal Palace by one Colonel George Gouraud, who worked as Thomas Edison's sales agent in Europe. This he did

"THE PERFORMANCES WERE COLOSSAL AND ONLY MADE POSSIBLE BY THE EXISTENCE OF THE RAILWAYS. AUDIENCES REGULARLY EXCEEDED 80,000."

using Edison's recently perfected phonograph. Placing the device 100 yards away, Gouraud succeeded in recording the chorus of 4,000 voices. This was one of the earliest recordings of music and voice ever made. Sadly, unlike the recording, the Crystal Palace did not survive. It was consumed by fire in 1936, despite the best efforts of 89 fire engines and 400 fire fighters. Over 100,000 people came to watch the final spectacle of the palace burning down.

The Great Exhibition of 1851 focused on all aspects of industry. In 1857, Manchester held an art treasures exhibition, displaying over 16,000 works of art. Similar in conception to the Great Exhibition, it ran from May to October, was housed in a building of cast iron and cast plate glass and attracted a great number of visitors. The temporary exhibition house was erected on a three-acre site at Old Trafford, an area of Manchester that had previously been leased to the city's cricket club. The club moved to the meadows of the de Trafford estate, where Old Trafford cricket ground still stands today.

The exhibition was served by the Manchester, South Junction and Altrincham Railway, which built a station named after the exhibition. The station is now the Old Trafford Tram Stop. The exhibition performed quite well commercially, making a small profit, but the railway did much

Old Trafford cricket ground in Manchester, circa July 1910.

better financially. Manchester had been made a city in 1853 and the art treasures exhibition announced its arrival on the world stage. It is still thought to be the largest exhibition of art ever held.

After the exhibition closed, the railway station continued to serve the cricket ground on match days. Old Trafford station serves as a reminder of the impact that the railways had on spectator sports. Old Trafford was the second venue to host test cricket in the United Kingdom. The first was the Oval in Kennington in London and not, as you might expect, the home of cricket, Lord's, which is situated north of the river.

The Oval had been a market garden owned by the duchy of Cornwall, but a lease was granted for the use of the site as a cricket ground. At the start of the nineteenth century, the piece of land in question would have been a relatively rural setting; however, by the close of the century it was a little island in the middle of a great industrial sprawl. That part of London almost remains a monument to the Victorian rail network, with lines criss-crossing each other as they spread out from Victoria and Waterloo. Then they funnel through Britain's busiest railway station, Clapham Junction, which was built in 1863 on an area of land that had previously seen the agricultural cultivation of lavender (hence the name 'Lavender Hill').

A panoramic view of the Kennington Oval cricket ground in London, early twentieth century.

The Oval was well suited to facilitate the arrival of the 20,000 spectators who came to see the first match of the first tour of England by any foreign side in 1868. The tourists were the Australian aboriginal cricket team, which played 47 matches in total across England, winning 14, losing 14 and drawing 19. They garnered the respect of the English players and introduced Britain to a wealth of culture. One English cricketer managed to narrowly win a cricket ball throwing competition against the aborigines with a 118-yard throw. He was the 20-year-old emerging talent, W. G. Grace.

The Oval – which is recognized as having the first floodlights of any sporting arena, in the form of gas lamps installed in 1889 – also witnessed the birth of the cricket competition known as the Ashes. What is now referred to as 'test cricket' had its origins in England's 1876–7 tour of New Zealand and Australia. However, it was a visit to England by Australia that saw the competition become immortalized. On average, it took 48 days to sail between the antipodes of Australia and the United Kingdom. Subsequently, the tourist team seldom consisted of a full compliment, as many of the best players could not be absent from work for so long. Perhaps the editor had that in mind when the *Sporting Times* published their mock obituary of English cricket, with a footnote stating 'the body will be cremated and the ashes taken to Australia'.

When England returned to Australia, the press – which had enjoyed increased circulations as a direct result of the railways – latched on to these mythical ashes and the statements being made that England would recover them. It took a number of years for the term to become fully ensconced in the *lingua franca* of cricket, but it is now one of the most famous sporting competitions in the world.

Like cricket, football owes much of its popularity to the railways. The football league was established in 1889 and the railways allowed spectators to travel both to home and away games. As the league grew and more teams became established, sites for grounds were often chosen based on their proximity to a railway. For example, Manchester United moved to Old Trafford in 1910, mainly to take advantage of the railway station that already served the cricket ground.

The London club Arsenal picked its former home at Highbury due to the proximity to Gillespie Road tube station; the ground of Tottenham Hotspur was deliberately situated close to White Hart Lane station; Chelsea picked a site near Waltham Green; and Wembley, which had been built for the British Empire Exhibition in 1924, was placed on a site with excellent rail links. The idea behind the British Empire Exhibition was that it should

The tiny urn that holds one of the greatest prizes in world sport – the Ashes.

The public debacle that was the 1923 FA cup football final at Wembley gave the authorities a great deal of pause for thought when it came to handling large crowds in the future.

feature a number of sites all linked by a circular railway, of which Wembley was one. The exhibition opened in 1923, just four days before the first event it was scheduled to host, the FA cup final. In the 51 years that the final had been staged, including eight replays, it was usually held in London. Two prominent venues for the event had been the Oval between 1874 and 1892 and the Crystal Palace between 1895 and 1914. It did not take place during the First World War and resumed in the 1919–1920 season.

Wembley stadium had an official capacity of 127,000, but the 1923 FA cup final was unticketed. This odd state of affairs was compounded by the organizers, who underestimated the number of fans who could turn up, due to the existence of the railways. There are no official figures available, but it is thought that the stadium was filled to at least double if not triple its official capacity (there were also a further 60,000 fans locked outside, to whom gate money had to be refunded). With many fans spilling out onto and almost covering the pitch, the match looked unlikely to take place, until mounted police cleared the playing area. The 1923 FA cup final is known to this day as the 'White Horse' final, due to the presence of the police horses that helped to clear the pitch prior to play commencing.

> **"THROUGHOUT HISTORY, LONDON HAS HAD A PROBLEM WITH DEATH, OR MORE ACCURATELY, WHAT TO DO WITH THE DEAD."**

Of the nine police horses that were involved, only one was in fact white – or 'grey', to use the correct equine terminology. Constable George Scorey and his white horse Billy helped push back the crowds, along with eight other mounted officers. However, due to Billy's distinctive colour, he stood out in the black and white photos of the event. As a result of the overcrowding, the match took place 45 minutes late. The bridge outside Wembley stadium was subsequently named in Billy's honour as 'White Horse Bridge'.

Although the 1923 FA cup final's unofficial attendance is probably the highest of any stadium-based sporting event ever, it does not compare to the crowds that regularly attended horse racing events. Cricket, football and boxing all benefited from increased attendances as a result of the railways. However, horse racing was already enormously popular and attracted huge local crowds. The railways just made them bigger. Perhaps part of the appeal of horse racing was that bets could be placed. The gaming act of 1845 meant that the only bets that could legally be placed were with turf accountants at the race tracks. Special excursion trains brought vast numbers of people to race meets across the country. Just before the Second World War, the amount of money being gambled on horse racing during the year was half a billion pounds. Bookies were legalized in 1961 by Harold Macmillan's government, perhaps as an attempt to collect the tax revenue.

LONDON'S BURIAL CRISIS

As the old saying goes, 'only two things are certain in life; death and taxes'. Throughout history, London has had a problem with death, or more accurately, what to do with the dead. Initially, those who died in the city were buried in church graveyards, but these became very crowded very quickly. The solution was more graveyards.

St George's Gardens in Bloomsbury is the site of the first Anglican burial ground that is set apart from a church. Opened in 1713, the park was originally comprised of two graveyards serving two churches – St George the Martyr on Queen's Street and St George's in Bloomsbury.

Brompton cemetery in Kensington, London, is typical of the Victorian burial grounds in the city that became completely over-subscribed during the nineteenth century.

The boundary between the two graveyards can be seen today, demarcated by a series of stones. However, St George's also ultimately became overcrowded.

The population of London recorded by the census of 1801 was under one million. The population of London in 1851 was just under 2.5 million. The amount of people dying in London was increasing exponentially, but the amount of space given over to graveyards was relatively unchanged. It was almost impossible to dig a fresh grave without cutting through existing graves. To make matters worse, the sheer number of corpses was beginning to pollute the water supply. From 1848 to 1849, there was a cholera epidemic in London and the bodies began quite literally to pile up. The system was totally overwhelmed, resulting in a crisis. In 1851, London's graveyards were closed to new internments. Something had to be done.

Inspired by Paris, between 1832 and 1842 London had embarked on creating seven large cemeteries outside the city limits. Now called the 'Magnificent Seven' – a term coined by the architectural historian Hugh Meller after the film of the same name – there was a worry that without a better solution these graveyards would also become overwhelmed. However, Richard Broun and Richard Sprye proposed using the railways as a means of transporting the deceased from central London to a large site well beyond the projected growth of the city in the years to come.

In 1852, the London Necropolis and National Mausoleum Company was established, following an act of Parliament, and on 7 November 1854

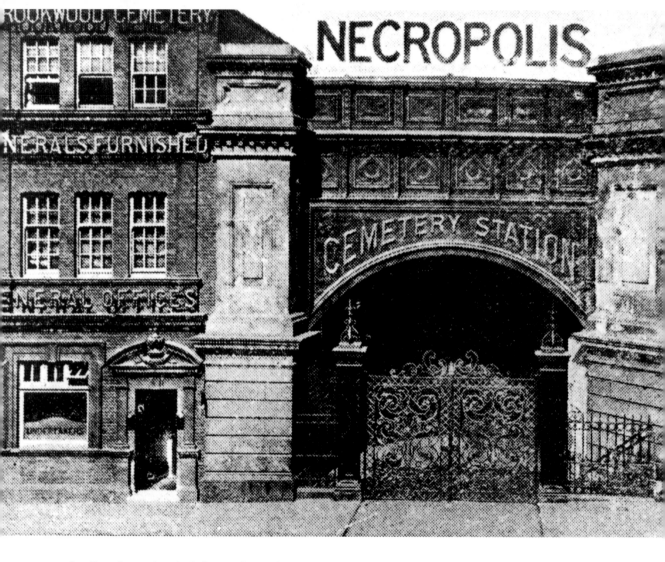

the first funeral train left London. The company, which simply became the London Necropolis Company in 1927, had a terminus station near Waterloo and another terminus station at Brookwood in Surrey, where it established what is still the UK's largest cemetery.

The plan was to run trains early in the morning and late at night, carrying the deceased along with their funeral party to the cemetery. The initial idea of moving the body and the mourners separately had been dismissed. The LNC anticipated moving tens of thousands of bodies a year, but this projection was never fulfilled. The LNC did, however, help relocate a lot of remains from existing London cemeteries. It was during the Victorian period that St George's graveyards in Bloomsbury were redesigned as gardens with the idea of creating an outdoor sitting room.

One train a day began running from the London Necropolis railway station to the Brookwood cemetery station. It used the London and South Western Railway line, which was subsequently linked onto the LNC's own branch lines at each end. The coffins and mourners were segmented in

The station built to handle the funeral traffic for the giant Necropolis cemetery at Brookwood in Surrey. When the Necropolis opened in 1854, it was intended to become London's only cemetery, as the city no longer had room to bury all of its dead.

upper or standard class. Upon arrival at the cemetery, the coffins were unloaded either at the north station for non-conformists, or the south station for Anglicans. There were also designated rooms for each class

> **"THE LSWR WERE QUITE WORRIED THAT THE IDEA OF THEIR LOCOMOTIVES PULLING DEAD BODIES MIGHT PUT OFF THEIR LIVING CUSTOMERS."**

of mourner. The initial design of the cemetery branch line meant that the engine would be at the wrong end of the train for the return trip. Therefore, near the entrance to the graveyard, the carriages were uncoupled and then pulled through the cemetery by a team of black horses.

The LSWR were quite worried that the idea of their locomotives pulling dead bodies might put off their living customers, so they bought steam engines specifically to pull the LNC trains. They also eventually provided a free lunch for their train crews (as long as only one beer was consumed by each man), after complaints that some train drivers became so drunk while waiting at the cemetery's licensed refreshment rooms that they were unable to drive the trains back.

The service ran daily until 1900, after which time it ran as required. The LNC trains stopped running in 1941 and the LNC railway ceased to operate altogether directly after the Second World War. The London Necropolis station had been destroyed in the blitz; the cemetery branch line needed the sleepers to be constantly replaced as the poor ground conditions accelerated their decay; and much of the rolling stock had also been lost in the war. When British Railways was formed in 1947, funeral trains went into steep decline. The last funeral train carried Lord Mountbatten in 1979, and in 1988 British Rail formally ceased carrying coffins altogether.

FAIRS AND MARKETS

OVERLEAF: **A traditional thatcher at work on a cottage roof in the British countryside. The fairs and markets that took place across Britain from the Middle Ages onwards celebrated many rural trades and occupations such as this.**

Thanks to steam and the network of railways, big events and day trips out became a part of many people's everyday lives – but it took time. Today, most people take a two-day weekend for granted, but the majority of Victorian working class people only had one day off – the Sabbath. This caused its own distinct set of problems.

The company that was initially set up to run the Crystal Palace when it first relocated did not open the venue on Sundays. This policy was in line

with the Lord's Day Observance Society's view that people, in this case staff at the palace, should not have to work on the Sabbath. However, starting in 1861, eventually the Crystal Palace began opening on a Sunday – and immediately enjoyed as many as 40,000 visitors in a day.

As society developed, so did social reform. Good Friday and Christmas Day had always been days of rest, but many of the other feast days associated with the religious calendar no longer applied to the working classes. The Bank of England reduced the number of saints' days it observed from thirty-three to four in 1834 (which included Good Friday and Christmas Day).

One banker who had a strong interest in reducing working hours for the working classes and the implementation of official holidays was John Lubbock. In 1871, he was instrumental in passing the Bank Holidays Act, while he was serving his first term as a Liberal MP. The days that applied to England, Wales and Ireland were Easter Monday, Whit Monday, the first Monday in August and St Stephen's Day (Boxing Day). The bank holidays were very popular and were initially referred to as 'St Lubbock days'.

Saints' days had played an important part in the British calendar since the Roman period. Many of them were associated with fairs or markets. Fairs played an important role in trade, with many being based upon a particular type of livestock. From the Middle Ages onwards, fairs and markets began to become established, as towns and villages were created.

Fairs are certainly known to have existed during the Roman period, when they were considered holidays. Markets and fairs crop up usually in association with a church and many were granted a royal charter. Chartered fairs, as they were known, reached their zenith in the thirteenth century and were an important outlet for trade and leisure in a community. When a fair or market was held, visitors would come from far and wide and the whole operation had to be policed.

Powers were granted to the fairs, so that courts could be held to enforce order and administer justice. These courts were known as 'piepowder courts', which directly translates as 'dusty feet courts', as a term applied to travellers who walked several miles to reach the fair. The last known piepowder court to be held was at the end of the nineteenth century in Hemel Hempstead, Hertfordshire, and the last active piepowder court was held at the Stag and Hounds public house on Market Street in Bristol. Although the court had not been held since 1870, it was officially abolished with the courts act in 1971.

The number of fairs diminished after the thirteenth century, as the number of markets settled down. However, the remaining fairs played

Smithfields Market in central London, which was inaugurated in 1798. This was a notoriously crowded and filthy public gathering place.

OVERLEAF: A carousel at a fair at Riddings, Derbyshire, circa 1900. Mechanical fairground rides became immensely popular in late Victorian and Edwardian society.

an important role in agriculture, as farmers and drovers moved livestock from hillside to fair along well-established drove roads. As the railways were developed and Britain became industrialized, many of the smaller fairs and markets ceased to exist. Livestock was primarily moved long distance by railway, but the larger markets flourished, such as Smithfields in London.

In certain places, fairs took on new life with industrialization. Famously, Glasgow fair has been held on the last fortnight in July since the twelfth century. Originally a livestock market focusing on the sale of horses and cattle and held at Glasgow cathedral, from the nineteenth century onwards it has been held at Glasgow Green and has become a beacon for travelling showmen. Incidentally, it has been stated that it was while walking in Glasgow Green that James Watt thought up his idea of a separate condenser and thereby made the Newcomen engine far more efficient and considerably more practical.

As the Glasgow fair was a holiday that was already well established in the fabric of the community, the factories in Glasgow respected fair Friday and shut down, to allow the workers to go to the celebrations at Glasgow Green. Fairs throughout history would have attracted travelling

> "LIVESTOCK WAS PRIMARILY MOVED LONG DISTANCE BY RAILWAY."

showmen. With the invention of steam, the fairs became mechanized and many of the showmen brought engines. Showmen engines were usually characterized by their bright colours and long canopies, which covered the whole engine. They had long or extendable chimneys to get the draw needed and to protect the punters from hot smuts. The engines were used to provide power for electric lighting and to operate rides.

As the steam power took hold, the rides took off. They became progressively bigger and would have changed the feel of the fairs from the agricultural affairs they once were to the funfairs and carnivals we know today. A 'carnival' was specifically a festival that happened directly before lent but, certainly in the UK, this has also become a term that is used to describe the annual town celebrations that were once fairs. One of the most enduring and popular rides at a fair is the carousel. It was invented by one Frederick Savage, who made the move from agricultural machine builder to fairground ride innovator. The name 'carousel' was derived from a complex military dressage manoeuvre that garnered popularity in medieval jousting arenas.

Shortly after seeing a mechanical steam-powered roundabout at the Aylesham fair in Norfolk, Frederick Savage began designing his fairground rides. By the turn of the century, he had perfected his carousel with lights, an organ and horses that galloped up and down on poles. These original carousels are things of beauty. Strangely, there has long been a tradition that British carousels rotate clockwise, whereas European and American carousels rotate anti-clockwise.

The practice of shutting the factories in Glasgow for the fair was not unique to that city. Many industrialized cities had similar traditions. There are a number of documented instances of factory fortnights or what are also termed 'wake weeks'. My mum can remember the factories all closing down at the same time when she was a girl growing up in Glasgow. She also remembers that the nearby cities would also shut their factories, but the dates would be staggered so as not to clash with those of Glasgow or other nearby industrial centres.

The roots of these factory fortnights lay both in the religious fairs and the Scottish tradition of the trades fortnight, when each trade takes its summer holiday. The usually unpaid leave of a wake week allowed the factories to undertake any maintenance jobs that could not be done while the factory was in steam, and it also allowed the factory workers to go on holiday. With the rail network in place, a holiday could be taken effectively anywhere, but the most popular destinations were the seaside resorts.

HOLIDAYS

The idea that the sea had restorative properties was a long and widely held belief. However, prior to the happy combination of both free time and the new access provided by the railways, a trip to the seaside had largely been the preserve of the rich. During the down time of a wake week, people would often travel to the seaside either as a day trip or later for an extended period. It was not until the Holiday Pay Act of 1938, following lobbying since the First World War, that wages were paid to the working classes during a vacation of the factory. Prior to that, savings clubs were set up to fund the excursions.

The landscapes of many of Britain's seaside towns have developed as a direct result of catering for the mass influx of tourists. Those settlements on the coast that have natural or manmade harbours that permit boats to dock were less affected, as they already had a rich culture of fishing

WILLIAM WORDSWORTH (1770–1850)

The poet William Wordsworth was not a fan of railways. When a proposal was made to extend the line to his beloved Lake Windermere, he fired off an extremely huffy letter of opposition to the *Morning Post* in 1844 with an even more disgruntled follow-up shortly after. His career as a poet had been spent extolling the beauty of the Lake District's wild places, in describing the solace such landscapes could bring. He strove, along with others, to change the public view of unproductive land from 'waste' to 'healing nature'. He wrote of the power of the wild natural world to inspire, to transport the human mind to a higher, more spiritual state. He wished people to follow his lead and head outside in search of the 'sublime'. But not, it transpires, too many people, or the wrong sort of people.

'We should have the whole of Lancashire, and no small part of Yorkshire, pouring in upon us to meet the men of Durham, and the borders from Cumberland and Northumberland. Alas, alas, if the lakes are to pay this penalty for their own attractions!

Picturesque and romantic scenery is so far from being intuitive, that it can only be produced by a slow and gradual process of culture; and ... as a consequence, that the humbler ranks of society are not, and cannot be, in a state to gain material benefit from a more speedy access than they now have to this beautiful region.'

Wordsworth's vision of the Lake District was one that he intended only for the select few.

However, the great British public read his poetry and took it to heart – and then they just as firmly ignored his letters about the unstoppable spread of the railways. Taking the train to outdoor beauty spots and making holidays from a mixture of train rides and walks, quickly and quietly became a nationwide habit – one enjoyed by all but the very poorest levels of society.

The promenade and tower, Blackpool, Lancashire, pictured in 1895.

and therefore an infrastructure built around an industry. However, many of Britain's beautiful beaches became beacons for visitors, and much of what can be seen in relation to a beach resort today was built in the Victorian period.

Blackpool is the most famous example of the seaside resort towns that boomed because of the railways. Trains from Preston brought wave after wave of tourists, primarily from Lancashire, along a branch line built in 1846. The staggering of mill and factory closures over the summer meant that Blackpool could both handle the tourists and was assured of a season. It had originally been a location for 'taking the cure', so some hotels did exist as well as a road to the resort. However, the trains brought huge numbers of tourists and that created a market that enterprising business people jumped upon. No longer would a dip in the sea and a game of bowls suffice.

Preston was the first location outside of London to have gas street lighting in 1825, and piped water was installed in 1864. Blackpool received gas lighting in 1852. The street lighting was upgraded to electric

The Great Wheel, Blackpool, Lancashire, 1890–1910. A view across the rooftops towards the Great Wheel beside the Winter Gardens in Blackpool. The wheel was erected at the end of the nineteenth century on the corner of Adelaide Street and Coronation Street.

street lighting in 1879, a year after Paris and London had seen some electric street lights. These lights along the promenade were associated with a certain amount of pageantry and spectacle, which later evolved into the world-famous Blackpool illuminations. In 1885, one of the world's first practical electric tramways was installed and ran with an unbroken history until 2012, when the rolling stock was upgraded. The old trams still run occasionally, and are some of the only double-decker trams in the world.

Blackpool also saw three piers constructed, the first being what is now north pier in 1863, central pier in 1868 and finally south pier in 1893, as the linear town of Blackpool spread further than the area known as the 'Golden Mile'. The Victorians constructed a lot of piers at seaside towns, but Blackpool is the only one to have three. Their design is in part due to the fact that when the tide goes out, often the promenade is a long way from the sea. Southend at the mouth of the river Thames has the longest pier in the world. It is 1.34 miles long, which reflects the fact that the sea goes out over a mile at low tide, exposing unattractive mud flats. If daytrippers are only visiting for a short time, a pier ensures good access to the sea. It also allows boats

OVERLEAF: The sun sets over the Bristol Channel behind the Victorian pier at Clevedon in Somerset.

SEEING THE SIGHTS

If you have ever read Jane Austen's *Pride and Prejudice*, you will know that by 1813 when the book was published, there was already a well established tourist tradition of visiting stately homes and picturesque countryside. Elizabeth Bennet, the heroine of the book, is taken on holiday by her aunt and uncle in their carriage, stopping at country inns along the way. They pay a visit to Pemberley, the grand home of Mr Darcy, and are shown around by the housekeeper. It was not an unusual thing to do – anyone who was well dressed and owned or could hire a carriage was free to make a similar visit by appointment to most of the great houses of Britain. However, getting there did limit the experience to the very top rungs of society. The railways were to change all that, allowing many more people the opportunity to partake of these upper-class pleasures. Up and down the country, wherever a line ran close enough, housekeepers began to find themselves inundated with requests. Regular hours for visiting began to be introduced and dedicated guides rather than the busy housekeeper were employed to look after this new flood of visitors.

Outdoor sites proved even more accessible. Consider Corfe Castle in Dorset, for example. At the end of the eighteenth century, it was attracting a trickle of romanticaly minded, well-heeled visitors – people like William Turner, who painted a watercolour of the scene in 1793, dwelling on the play of light across its crumbling ivy-clad walls. It was just the sort of place that Elizabeth Bennet would have visited had her holiday been in Dorset rather than Derbyshire and by 1829 sported its own guide book, *A Historical and Architectural Description of Corfe Castle By a Near Neighbour*, which was full of historical colour and atmosphere. In 1885, a new branchline opened from Wareham to Swanage, passing right alongside the castle with a station at its foot. The latest guidebook published just eighteen months earlier – *The History and Description of Corfe Castle*, by Thomas Bond – began '*The silence of this gloomy fortress has rarely been disturbed save by the wail of the captive in his dungeon, or the clank of the warder, as he paced his rounds within the battlements.*' It was a rather serious booklet in the main, outlining the author Thomas Bond's 'diggings' (archaeology of a sort) and historical researches among the records, but he could not resist the gothic, the romantic and the emotive. Such sites were meant to be enjoyed on several levels and ever-increasing numbers of people arrived by rail to walk, to admire the view, to dream romantic dreams, to enjoy the puzzle of working out the architecture and to feel a connection with the past. The low-cost nature of such sights was an additional draw.

By 1935, the Southern Railway was using an image of Corfe Castle with the railway running around its base upon posters to advertise their services. Visiting historic monuments and scenic countryside generated good passenger income.

such as paddle steamers to dock without the need for a harbour, and bring visitors to the towns via the sea.

Piers for the loading and unloading of cargo have been around for a long time, but in the nineteenth century pleasure piers were an entirely new thing. Blackpool north pier is the longest of the three piers and was originally only intended as a promenade. It was built near to the first, and now only, railway station. As the town grew, central pier was built five years after the construction of Blackpool Hounds Hill railway

station (later Blackpool central) which at its peak had 14 platforms and was the station with the most platforms to close in the 1964 revision of the railways. Both piers offered steamboat excursions, but central pier focused on fun – mainly in the form of dancing – rather than the more genteel pursuits offered by north pier. When south pier was built, north and central piers were competing for that 'fun' tourist market. South pier was commissioned when people began going further down to south shore, after a carousel was installed near the sand dunes. It was wider and shorter than its predecessors, had 36 shops, a bandstand, an ice cream parlour and a photo booth. It is also where the popular twentieth century entertainer Harry Corbett bought the famous television show glove puppet that was known as Sooty.

Blackpool's physical attractions also include: the Winter Gardens, built in 1878; the pleasure beach, first started in 1896 opposite the tram terminus, but which came into its own in the early twentieth century; and, most famously, the Blackpool tower, which opened in 1894. Designed to look like the Eiffel Tower, it stands at 158 metres tall and is a monument to the evolution and development of coastal towns due to the railways.

Holidaymakers and daytrippers from Glasgow often found themselves in the nearby coastal resort of Millport. To get there, the tourists would generally travel down the Clyde on a paddle steamer. Millport still sees the last operational sea-going passenger paddle steamer, the *Waverley*, visiting the resort and bringing passengers in the summer. The PS *Waverley* was built in 1946 to replace a previous paddle steamer named *Waverley*. That ship was built in 1899 and saw service as a minesweeper in the Second World War, before being sunk during the evacuation of Dunkirk in 1940. She was part of the LNER and worked their Firth of Clyde steamer route briefly, before the nationalization of the railways, when she came under control of the railway executive. The notation 'PS' stands for 'paddle steamer', which is a vessel with a large paddle wheel

The *Comet* – the first English steamboat – conceived and constructed by Henry Bell in 1812.

on the side. 'SS' stood for 'screw steamer', which is a vessel with a propeller, although SS often just means 'steam ship'.

It was on the Firth of Clyde in 1812 that Henry Bell's *Comet* ran as the first

> **"UNLIKE SHIPS THAT PURELY RELIED ON SAIL, STEAM-POWERED VESSELS COULD STILL PROGRESS WHEN THERE WAS INSUFFICIENT WIND."**

commercially successful steamboat service in Europe. By 1822, there were 50 steamers in operation on the Clyde and by 1900 there were over 300. Steam power on the rivers and more importantly the seas allowed for boat services to be run in much the same vein as the railways. Unlike ships that purely relied on sail, steam-powered vessels could still progress when there was insufficient wind. Although affected by adverse weather, on the whole they could be run on a timetable. The great Victorian engineer Isambard Kingdom Brunel was commissioned as chief engineer to build the Great Western Railway in 1833. He envisioned a steam ship service from Bristol to New York that could effectively be an extension of the railway. In 1836, the Great Western Steam Ship Company was established, and from 1838 until 1846 a regular transatlantic service ensued.

The Great Western Steam Ship Company was affected by the rocky debut of Brunel's SS *Great Britain*. Initially intended to be a paddle steamer, Brunel changed the design after seeing the SS *Archimedes*, the first screw-propelled steam ship. When floated in 1843, the SS *Great*

Britain was the largest vessel on the seas. However, her extended build time and increasing costs had taken their toll on the company. When she ran aground due to navigational error and was feared beyond retrieval, the Great Western Steam Ship Company suspended all sailings and went out of business in 1846.

The SS *Great Britain* was however saved, and continued in service for several more years as a steam passenger ship with Gibbs, Bright & Co. While in operation as a passenger ship, she ferried the England cricket team on their first tour of Australia in 1861. She was then converted to a sailing ship to carry cargo, in 1882. She is now a museum in dry dock in her home town of Bristol.

Steam ships and railways linking the world are ultimately what ended the existing upper class tradition of the Grand Tour. They also changed it to create something that was cheaper, easier and open to all. Mass tourism was now a realistic option and one man was ready and waiting to make it happen – Thomas Cook.

British steamship SS *Great Britain*, depicted in 1847. Designed by Isambard Kingdom Brunel, she was the first screw-propelled iron vessel to cross the Atlantic. SS *Great Britain* was completed in Bristol in 1845 and provided accommodation for about 360 passengers.

Thomas Cook is considered to have been the first commercial tour operator. He started by offering day excursions to the temperance society to which he belonged. The excursions were to events including the Great Exhibition in 1851. Excursions that were cheap, popular and conveyed large groups to a single event were pioneered by the Mechanics Institute, which in 1841 organized visits between the Leicester and Nottingham branches. These excursions were many people's first experience of train travel and moving at speed and were quite the spectacle themselves, with most of the townsfolk waving the trains off.

Cook's excursions quickly established him as a popular tour operator, and by 1855 he was organizing tours to Europe. Starting with the Paris exhibition, his plan was to offer grand circular tours of Europe and then further afield, as 'inclusive independent travel'. By the mid-1860s, Cook's tours were taking in Egypt and America. Thomas Cook was joined by his son John Mason Cook, and in 1871 the company became Thomas Cook & Son, offering round the world tours that took in Japan, China and India.

The company published Cook's continental timetable, which they continued to print up until 2013. It is now printed by a different company. In 1874 the company began issuing circular cheques, which are now better known by their AmEx branded name of 'traveller's cheques'. Thomas Cook & Son established offices around the world and in 1888 they sold three and a quarter million tickets for package holidays.

The tours were relatively expensive and lasted several weeks, but they were a once in a lifetime event and catered very much for the emerging middle classes. While on tour, excursions were offered that took in local culture or activities. The company also published guidebooks for travellers and they sold paraphernalia in their shops that prospective travellers might need, such as luggage and suitable footwear.

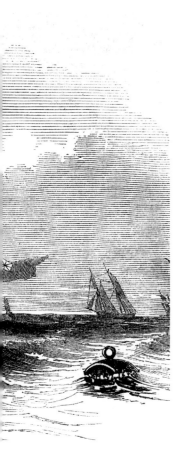

ABOVE RIGHT: **English tourist pioneer Thomas Cook (1808–1892).**

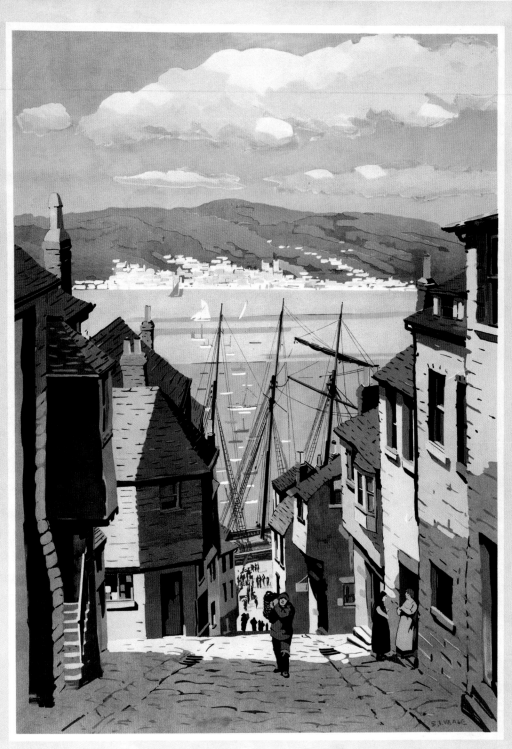

COME TO OLD WORLD
CORNWALL
Great Western Railway

As mass travel now became available through the power of steam, certain destinations gained a new clientele. Nice in the south of France near the border with Italy was one such place, adopted by the

> **"THE RAILWAYS FACILITATED TRAVEL ACROSS THE WORLD AND WITH IT CAME SOME ICONIC TRAINS, SUCH AS THE ORIENT EXPRESS AND THE BLUE TRAIN."**

British as a location to take the winter sun. With money donated by the Reverend Lewis Way, a promenade was built in Nice that was named the Promenade des Anglais. Similarly, in the north of France, Dinard became a very popular destination for summer holidaymakers, and in the late nineteenth century wealthy Britons built large villas along the coast.

The railways facilitated travel across the world and with it came some iconic trains. The Orient Express, the Trans-Siberian railway and the Blue Train are all examples of the grandeur put on offer by many of the world's railway companies. The Orient Express is perhaps most famous because of the Agatha Christie novel, *Murder on the Orient Express*. It became a byword for luxury, but in reality it was a rail service that primarily linked Paris with Istanbul. The Blue Train was a luxury overnight express favoured by the wealthy that linked Calais with the French riviera. To link up to these, Southern Railway offered the Golden Arrow, which carried passengers to Dover and onto a luxury boat service to Calais. From there a connection to Paris could be taken, in the form of the equivalent *Flèche d'Or*.

Holidays were not a reality for all, but a tradition of hop-picking as a working holiday was cultivated by the railways. Beer was an essential drink in places where there was no source of reliable clean water. The boiling of the water, the alcohol and the hops all added to its preservative and sterile characteristics. One place that beer was required was India, but traditional brews did not travel well. The solution was the development of the IPA or Indian Pale Ale, which had both a slightly higher alcohol content and an increased number of hops that contain natural antiseptics.

Hop-picking today is generally mechanized, but before these innovations it was a labour intensive process. At one point hops were grown across the entire country and would have been harvested by seasonal workers to be used by the local breweries. However, as the railways were

OPPOSITE: For those who could afford the train ticket, suddenly far-flung destinations such as Cornwall – or even more exotic climes abroad – were within reach.

developed, farming could become specialized and suddenly breweries could get their hops from Kent and their barley from Hampshire, if they so desired. The railways meant that counties that grew large numbers of hops could bring in large numbers of seasonal workers in a process that developed into working holidays for the working classes, especially those from the east end of London. The hops were picked, often using stilts for the large climbing varieties, put into bags while still green, and taken to drying houses. Once dried, the hops were packaged into large sacks known as hop pockets and then transported to the breweries. The sacks were a good six feet long and weighed about 80 kilograms. A few hops go a long way in the brewing process, as they are very pungent and act like a herb in cooking. However, due to the vast quantities of beer being produced and either sold or given as a daily ration to those working in industrial environments, such as metal-producing factories, the demand for hops remained high.

The train remained a leading form of transport for holidays up until the advent of affordable air travel, although at the end of the nineteenth century touring cars were beginning to appear. In 1900, the French tyre manufacturing company Michelin produced a restaurant guide for motorists so that they could determine if a restaurant was worth a detour. The guide was given away for free in France and was intended to boost the demand for cars and subsequently car tyres.

Although the internal combustion engine fuelled by petrol became the primary car propulsion system, there were other forms of car being made, including steam cars. For a short period in history, steam cars represented the pre-eminent car technology. The knowledge that had been gained and refined through the operation of steam engines on the railways meant that the first steam cars had advantages over their internal combustion engine competitors. They were very quiet and their fires consumed most pollutants, so there were fewer emissions. They did not require a crank handle to start them and they could be driven off quickly once they were at operating temperature. Innovations in steam motoring technology saw some steam cars being able to start from cold after forty seconds of the turn of a key. Like the steam locomotives on the railways, steam cars did not require complex transmission systems and so did not need a clutch. Incredibly, for a while, a steam car even held the land speed record.

However, steam cars did have drawbacks – primarily their vast consumption of water. Some cars had facilities to carry extra fuel and water, but when the electric starter motor was introduced along with

"ONCE DRIED, THE HOPS WERE PACKAGED INTO LARGE SACKS AND TAKEN TO THE BREWERIES."

For those of lesser means, a working holiday spent hop-picking in the fields of Kent was often an agreeable option.

OVERLEAF: Steam enthusiasts demonstrate their engines at the Great Dorset Steam Fair, the biggest event of its kind in Europe, September 2011, Tarrant Hinton, near Blandford, Dorset, England.

the production line, both the ease and the cost of petrol cars improved. After the Great War, steam cars started to become museum pieces and collectables for enthusiasts. Like steam locomotives, they are remembered fondly as part of a world that no longer exists.

MEMORABILIA

Due to the pollution that they caused – 'peasouper' fogs in London and smog that enveloped many other cities – in the end steam engines were viewed by many as dirty and inefficient. However, steam engines are a marvel, and during their heyday and after their time they have captured the imaginations of many and taken a permanent residence in that world of nostalgia and memorabilia.

The decision taken in 1955 to stop steam engines on the railways actually did not come into effect until the summer of 1968. One year later, in the summer of 1969, what is now known as the Great Dorset Steam Fair was launched. Although its focus is not on the steam engines of the railways but rather on the traction engines used in agriculture and on the roads, it is a demonstration of the British public's love of steam, with its regular annual visitors numbering as many as 200,000 people.

The idea of preserving steam has been around since the early steam locomotives were gradually being superseded. A proposal for a national

railway museum was made in the nineteenth century and the Science Museum inherited an early collection of steam engines that was started by the patent office in the 1860s. Several of the railway companies kept examples of their early innovations on display at stations, but it was hit and miss as to what was preserved and how well it was preserved.

Commander John Baldock began collecting traction engines in the 1940s, as they began to disappear from everyday life. At times, traction engines would be pulled out of hedges where they had been abandoned in favour of new machines, but now they are now worth a lot of money. Baldock's collection grew and became what is now the Hollycombe steam collection, based near the town of Liphook in Hampshire. It consists of agricultural, fairground and railway machinery, which without museums, enthusiasts and collectors would have faded from life only to exist in art and fleeting glimpses in films.

Railways have always lent themselves well to film and the public imagination. Cinematography started in the 1890s and took off from there. Prior to 1927, films were silent, accompanied by an organist, pianist or even an orchestra. They are a visual medium that can document motion beautifully, so trains have always been a natural fit for the silver screen.

Peter Ginn and Alex Langlands posing in front of the traction engine *Oberon* while crushing stone for ballast.

A 1951 poster for the classic Alfred Hitchcock film, *Strangers on a Train*.

The showing of the world's first public film at the Grand Café in Paris contained a railway scene. Soon after, the short films of around one minute that could be made with the early technology featured aspects of the railways, such as trains passing or expresses arriving at stations. In the late 1890s, a number of films termed 'phantom rides' were made, by strapping the camera to the front of the locomotive and effectively filming the dramatic point of view of the locomotive.

ALFRED HITCHCOCK
HAS A NEW ANGLE ON A MATTER OF EXPRESS URGENCY

STRANGERS ON A TRAIN

STARRING
FARLEY **GRANGER** · RUTH **ROMAN** · ROBERT **WALKER**

As the cinematic technology progressed, so too did the sophistication of how the trains were used. *Strangers on a Train*, *The Great Locomotive Chase*, *Paris Express* – in all these films, the train was the star. A film made in 1979 called *The First Great Train Robbery* was based on the book by Michael Crichton, which in turn is based on the actual events of the great gold robbery in 1855. During this great crime, gold en route from London to Paris was stolen and substituted by lead shot, so that the crime would remain undetected until the lead had reached the continent. Crichton's version contains a theory by the robbers that when exiting the moving train to climb back to the guard's van, the prevailing forces created by the moving train would help anchor the villains to the train. A nice insight into the Victorian mindset regarding a new technology. It could be argued that, in part, trains helped attract audiences to cinemas, as they were so monumental in society.

Trainspotting is a term that many find offensive and can have a variety of different connotations. What is definite is that with steam locomotives came a fascination of steam engines, most usually amongst small boys. Springburn in Glasgow, Scotland – where my mother grew up – was a rural hamlet at the start of the nineteenth century, as the name might suggest.

> **"RAILWAYS HAVE ALWAYS LENT THEMSELVES WELL TO FILM."**

> **"WHEN AN ENGINE WAS COMPLETED, IT WAS BROUGHT OUT OF THE RESPECTIVE WORKS FOR TRANSPORT ON TO ITS INTENDED DESTINATION."**

However, by the end of the nineteenth century, it was an inner city district. It was home to heavy industry associated with the railways, with four railway manufacturing sites. At one time it was producing 25 per cent of the world's locomotives. Often the locomotives were for domestic usage, but many were for use overseas, and Springburn built some giants. When an engine was completed, it was brought out of the respective works and into the streets for transport on to its intended destination. This was a spectacle not to be missed by the children playing in the streets, especially the boys.

It is perhaps the unique nature of steam engines, their varied personalities and how much they impacted people's lives that fostered a national obsession with trains. Ian Allan worked in the PR department of Southern Railways at the age of twenty in the offices of Waterloo station. He received various requests by interested members of the public as to the extent of Southern Railway's rolling stock. Taking the initiative, he published *The ABC of Southern Locomotives*, which proved so popular that he formed an eponymous publishing company to simultaneously create and promote the hobby of trainspotting.

Trainspotting is still going strong today and is often accompanied by train photography. Many railway enthusiasts also pursue the hobby of creating model railways. The first model railways available were toys from the 1840s. There was no track and they were known as 'carpet railways' or 'Birmingham dribblers'. The locomotive was operated by steam and could run along the floor. A number exploded, so later models had safety valves fitted. Carpet railways were produced by a number of companies and ran on the burning of methylated spirits, which would have been readily available as a source of fuel for lamps. Their wheels could be turned so that the engine would run in a circle without the need for track.

Model railways are serious business. A magazine published in 1898 called *Model Engineer* provided literature for the emerging hobby and is still published today. The oldest society in Britain for enthusiasts is the Model Railway Club near King's Cross in London and was established in 1910. There are a number of gauges or scales that are used for modelling

OVERLEAF: **Peter Ginn and friends delivering beer barrels with the traction engine *Tiger*.**

Presenters Peter Ginn and Alex Langlands posing by slate wagons on the narrow-gauge preserved railway line at Ffestiniog in northwest Wales.

and often entire dioramas of specific periods of history of certain railways are recreated. Some scales – such as the 1972 Z scale – mean the locomotives can be held in the palm of the hand, and other scales – such as the live steam 1:8 scale – allow for the creation of an actual ride on the railways.

Model railways are not considered toys, but it was quickly realized that there was a market that stood somewhere between the accurate scaling and recreating of railways and playing with a 'Birmingham dribbler'. Frank Hornby, who had invented and patented Mechano in 1901 and successfully improved it by 1907, began making train sets in 1920. They were initially clockwork, but the firm that Hornby set up was soon producing electric train sets. They began making models on the 00 gauge in 1938 and since then this has remained Britain's most popular model gauge.

Steam fairs, museums and model railways are all good sources of information about the era of steam trains, but it is the preserved railways that keep much of our knowledge of Britain's steam railway heritage alive. Many of Britain's preserved railways were established shortly after the axe of Dr Beeching fell in the 1960s. This has led to a strange situation in which some railways are close to operating longer as preserved railways than they did originally as commercial railways, and some rolling stock has had a longer working life in the heritage world than it did when it was first built.

There are over 170 preserved heritage railways in the UK and Ireland, focusing on all aspects of Britain's railways. These include post-steam projects such as the Advanced Passenger Train and the mighty diesels known as the 'deltics'. Some lines, such as the Ffestiniog railway in northwest Wales, are narrow gauge industrial lines. Ffestiniog grew up around the slate mining industry and cuts through the beautiful Snowdonian landscape. Others are branch lines. The Keighley and Worth Valley railway in West Yorkshire is quite unique in that it is an entire branch line. Most preserved railways tend to be one end of the other of a discontinued branch and often, if they have two parts of a branch line, they have grand plans of linking them up. The only preserved double track mainline railway is the Great Central Railway in Leicestershire. Most steam railways are limited to 25mph, but the Great Central Railway breaks this rule as its trains travel at over 35mph. This is due to their operation of the travelling post office. The leather pouches that contain the mail that are hung off the side of the train or snatched up by the net on the side of the train will only work at between 35mph and 85mph. If the train is travelling more slowly, the mechanism will buckle and become damaged.

Knowledge is lost very quickly after something stops happening. The creation of Britain's railways changed the world and continues to have a profound effect on our lives. Steam railways facilitated leisure time and gave us the impetus for mass travel. With those systems in place, the airlines took up the baton of package holidays from the mid-1960s onwards, and with the advent of cheap air travel many of the towns that had thrived under the railways, such as Blackpool, began to decline. However, railways still afford us the opportunity of moving quickly across the country and the world. We still use railways for leisure, be it to attend a football match, to listen to bands play in a muddy field in the countryside, or to have a city break.

The innovations and ideas of the nineteenth century still shape our leisure time and many of those railways that closed have found new life as tracks for walkers. One example is the Parkland walk in London, which was the old railway that used to connect Finsbury Park with Alexandria Palace. It is quite evident, due to its location in such an urban area. Other former railway lines are often stumbled upon in the countryside. Mainly firm under foot, generally level and often passing under or over bridges, the telltale signs that a linear lane was once a branch line are all around. Next time you stroll down one, have a think about just how much work went into its creation and just how much the railways forged British society.

> **"THE CREATION OF BRITAIN'S RAILWAYS CHANGED THE WORLD."**

INDEX,
ACKNOWLEDGEMENTS
AND PICTURE
CREDITS

INDEX

ACKNOWLEDGEMENTS

We are a small team that has had the privilege of working together for many years. We are very lucky in the people we have met during this project and all their efforts in making this series on the history of the steam railways a reality. There are too many people to mention and we sincerely thank everyone who has been involved in some way. However, below are just some of the names of the crew, the preservation railways, the locations, organizations and individuals who have made this series possible.

Alex Langlands
Donna Clark
Nick Catliff
Richard Bradley
Claire Smith
Stuart Elliott
Chris Mitchell
Tom Pilbeam
George Stewart
Emma Randle-Caprez
Rachael Pagget
Tim Hodge and Henry Dog
Bill Rudolf
Steve Brown
Dominic Hutton
Anne Shanley
Felicia Gold
Fjolla Iberhysaj
Charlotte Lee
Emma Murie
Simon Bradley
Colin Richards and family
The porth-y-waen basalt quarry
Julie-Marie Strange
Brian Allison
Milton Keynes Museum
Gunton Sawmill
Gunton Park
Keighley & Worth Valley Railway
Ffestiniog & Welsh Highland Railways
Bonkers
Llechwedd Caverns
Tickle the horse (and owners)
Edward Crouch
Keith Payne
Matt Sears
Watercress Line
John Boyd Textiles
Great Central Railway
Bradle Farm

Museum of Rail Travel
Portland Basin Museum
Sue Day, Crew and Bilbo
Hal and Guy Debes
Foxfield Railway
Fortunes Kippers
Beamish Museum
Quarry Bank Mill
National Railway Museum
Flying Scotsman
Steam Dreams
Madame Tussauds
Fosters Shoe Shop
Lock & Co
James Smith & Sons
Devon Cattle Show
Borough Market
Kings Cross Station
St Pancras Station
Holkham Hall
Carter's steam fair
Kimmeridge Beach
Simon Penn
Swanage Railway
Speyside Cooperage
Ballindalloch Distillery
South Devon Railway
Bluebell Line
Network Rail
Shepherd Neame Brewery
Gwili Railway
National Wool Museum, Wales
Wiltshire Museum
St Pancras Renaissance Hotel
Powysland Museum
David Turner
Dave Cope
John Martin
Andy Hole

PICTURE CREDITS